Psychology of DOODLES & SCRIBBLES

Visual Expression of the Unconscious

Saurabh Avasthi

Notion Press

Notion Press
USA | INDIA

Publisher:
Notion Press Media Pvt Ltd
#7, Red Cross Road,
Egmore, Chennai, Tamil Nadu 600008
Email ID: publish@notionpress.com
Phone Number: +91 44 46315631

Book Title:
Psychology of
DOODLES & SCRIBBLES:
VISUAL EXPRESSION OF THE UNCONSCIOUS

Genre: Psychology, Motivational Self-Help
Edition: 1, October 2023
Language: English
Country of Origin: India
Copyright © Author: Saurabh Avasthi

Other Books by Author:
Vedic Numerology || Ank Jyotish || The Proven Methodology to Accurate Prediction, 2023

The Art and Science of Signature Analysis: A Step-by-Step Guide to Deciphering Nature, Behavior, Personality and Intent, 2023

Encyclopedia of Graphology: A Master Practitioner's Guide - Volume I: Gestalt Method – Holistic Approach to Handwriting Analysis, 2023

Encyclopedia of Graphology: A Master Practitioner's Guide - Volume II: Trait Method – Feature Analysis Approach to Handwriting Analysis (Letters A to Z, Numerals), 2023

Basics of Graphology, 2023

Bespoke Sales Pitch: Date of Birth = Buying Behaviour = Sales Pitch, 2019

DEDICATED TO

To my dearest parents,
I. C. Awasthi and Kiran Awasthi

PREFACE

In the intricate dance between the conscious and the subconscious, the language of the mind finds a unique expression - a silent dialogue conveyed through the strokes of a pen, the curves of a line, and the patterns of a doodle. "Psychology of DOODLES & SCRIBBLES: Visual Expression of the Unconscious" delves into this enigmatic world, seeking to unravel the stories embedded in the seemingly spontaneous creations that grace the margins of our notebooks, the corners of our meeting agendas, and the edges of our day-to-day lives.

In the pages that follow, we navigate through the landscape of doodles and scribbles, exploring the hidden meanings behind trees, waves, hearts, animals, and a myriad of symbols that emerge when pen meets paper.

As we embark on this exploration together, let the pages of "DOODLES & SCRIBBLES" be a mirror reflecting the depths of your own psyche. May it inspire you to pick up a pen, embrace the beauty of expression, and unlock the secrets concealed within the lines and shapes that emerge from the reservoir of your unconscious mind.

Happy doodling!

Saurabh Avasthi

ACKNOWLEDGMENTS

In the pursuit of unraveling the mysteries embedded in the world of doodles, I am grateful to have the support and encouragement of some remarkable individuals.

First and foremost, I want to express my deepest gratitude to my wife Meenakshi Awasthi, whose support, insights, and encouragement have been invaluable in bringing this book to fruition.

My sincere thanks to my dear friend, Shailendra Kumar. Your unwavering belief in this project, insightful contributions, and continuous encouragement have been the pillars that sustained me throughout this journey. Your friendship is a constant source of inspiration.

To the students who have embarked on the fascinating journey of handwriting analysis with me, I extend my deepest appreciation. Your curiosity, questions, and commitment to learning have not only enriched my life but have also significantly influenced the content of this book.

Finally, to all the readers, enthusiasts, and practitioners who will delve into the pages of "Psychology of DOODLES & SCRIBBLES: Visual Expression of the Unconscious" your quest for knowledge is the driving force behind the evolution of this field. Thank you to each and every person who has played a part, big or small, in this incredible endeavor. Your contributions have left an indelible mark on the pages of this project.

With sincere gratitude,

Saurabh Awasthi

PROLOGUE

In the intricate mosaic of human expression, lies a realm often overlooked - the realm of doodles. As we navigate the pages of "Psychology of DOODLES & SCRIBBLES: Visual Expression of the Unconscious" we embark on a journey that transcends the limits of conscious thought, delving into the fascinating language of the unconscious mind.

This exploration is not just about idle scribbles on paper; it's an odyssey into the intricate web of symbols, shapes, and patterns that our subconscious weaves effortlessly. Doodles, those seemingly insignificant drawings, become windows through which we can peer into the hidden corridors of our thoughts, emotions, and desires.

As we unravel the symbolism behind trees, hearts, waves, and a myriad of other visual expressions, we unveil the subtle nuances of the human psyche.

"DOODLES & SCRIBBLES" is not merely a collection of interpretations; it's an invitation to introspection. It's a call to examine the patterns we unconsciously sketch and discover the profound meanings they carry. Join me in this exploration of the visual language that transcends cultural boundaries, revealing universal aspects of the human experience.

So, as you turn the pages, let your curiosity guide you, and may you find within these doodles a mirror reflecting the intricate landscapes of your own subconscious.

Welcome to the journey.

Saurabh Awasthi

Psychology of DOODLES & SCRIBBLES:

Visual Expression of the Unconscious

Suarabh Avasthi

Table of Contents

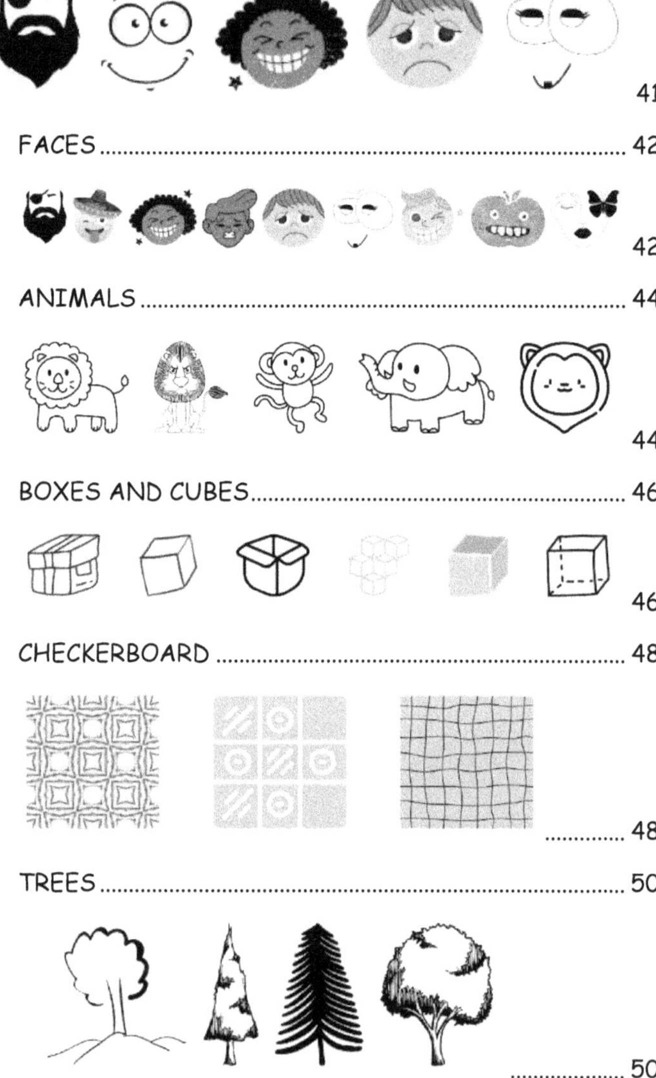

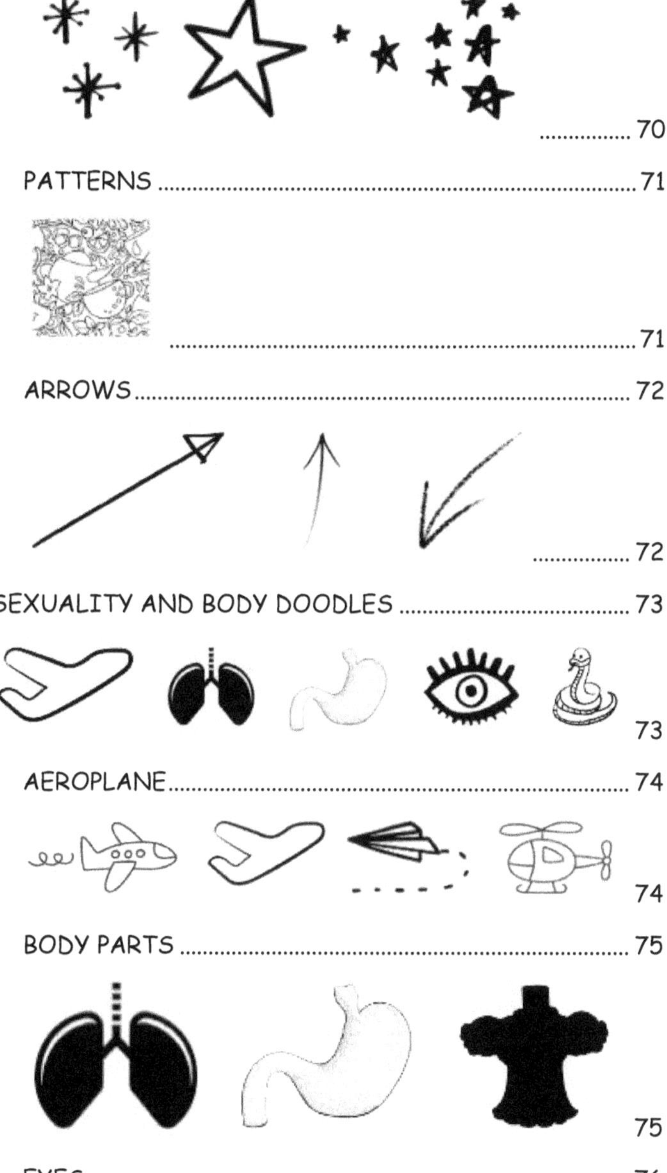

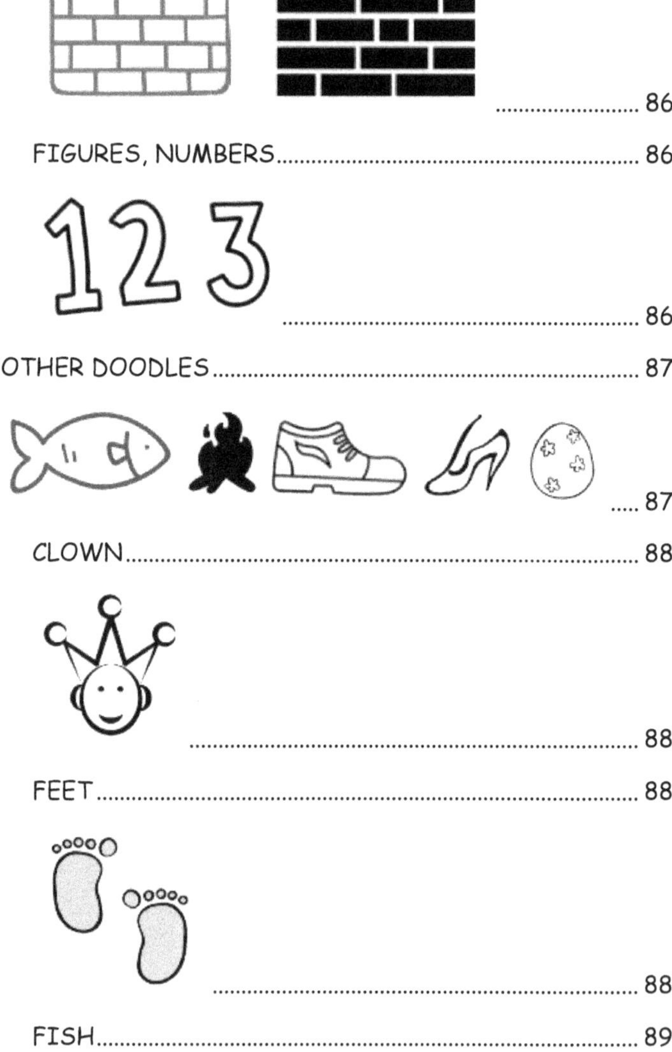

DOODLES – THE GRAPHIC EXPRESSION

Imagine a moment when you absentmindedly scribbled on a piece of paper while on the phone or lost in thought during a meeting. What seemed like idle marks actually held a deeper significance - those are doodles, and they offer a fascinating window into your unconscious mind. Doodling is the act of creating spontaneous, free-flowing drawings while your conscious mind is occupied elsewhere. These seemingly simple sketches are powerful tools that allow you to communicate and understand your thoughts, emotions, and desires on a level beyond words. Let's explore this concept further and delve into the relationship between doodles, the unconscious mind, and the age-old saying, "A picture paints a thousand words."

The Unconscious State in Doodling
Our unconscious mind is like a vast reservoir of thoughts, memories, emotions, and desires that often operate beneath our conscious awareness. Doodling taps into this rich realm. When you doodle, your conscious mind relaxes its hold, giving your unconscious thoughts a chance to surface. The lines, shapes, and patterns you create on paper are like fragments of your inner world, glimpses into the thoughts and emotions that might be too subtle to articulate verbally.

Example 1: Emotional Echoes: Consider doodling spirals while listening to music. The spirals might grow larger and more chaotic during intense parts of the song, mirroring the emotional journey the music takes you on. This doodle becomes a visual record of your emotional response.

Example 2: Mind Wandering: Doodling while your mind wanders during a lecture can lead to unexpected imagery. A doodle of a castle might emerge, indicating a mental escape to a world of daydreams - a snapshot of your unconscious mental trajectory.

A Picture Paints a Thousand Words

The saying "A picture paints a thousand words" encapsulates the idea that a single image can convey complex meanings more effectively than a multitude of words. Doodling embodies this concept; in the seemingly random lines, you encapsulate thoughts and emotions that could take paragraphs to describe verbally.

Example 1: Expressing Stress: A doodle of tangled lines might capture the feeling of being overwhelmed. While describing your stress verbally might take time, the doodle instantly communicates the inner turmoil you're experiencing.

Example 2: Capturing Creativity: During moments of inspiration, doodling can unleash creative energy. A doodle of intertwining shapes and patterns might symbolize the way different ideas are merging and intertwining in your mind.

The Journey of Self-Discovery

Doodling goes beyond a fleeting pastime; it's a form of self-discovery. By analyzing your doodles, you can decipher patterns, symbols, and emotions that reveal hidden aspects of your personality and experiences.

Example 1: Unveiling Desires: Drawing doodles of open roads and faraway places might indicate a desire for adventure and exploration. These symbols can serve as a roadmap to your dreams and aspirations.

Example 2: Confronting Fears: A doodle of a closed box might reflect feelings of confinement or a reluctance to open up emotionally. This simple drawing becomes a mirror that reflects a hidden fear or hesitation.

Doodles are the visual language of your unconscious mind, speaking in a code of shapes, lines, and symbols. Each doodle is a snapshot of your thoughts and feelings in a particular moment, an unfiltered glimpse into the inner workings of your mind. By understanding this concept and embracing doodling as a form of self-expression and exploration, you open the door to a richer understanding of yourself and a unique way to navigate the intricate landscape of your thoughts and emotions. So, the next time you pick up a pen and start to doodle, remember that you're creating more than just lines on paper - you're crafting a visual tapestry that weaves together the threads of your unconscious mind.

WHAT

Doodles, those seemingly random marks on paper, hold a fascinating world of their own. Unlike handwriting, which follows specific rules and forms recognizable letters, doodles are clusters of shapes, lines, dots, and squiggles that emerge spontaneously and repetitively.

The Essence of Doodling

Imagine sitting in a meeting or on a call, your mind partially engaged, when your hand starts moving, creating shapes, lines, and patterns without conscious intention. Those absentminded drawings are doodles. Doodling is an almost reflexive act - the hand moves almost independently, forming designs that can range from simple to intricate.

Example 1: The Classic Notebook Doodle: During a long lecture, you might find yourself unconsciously sketching tiny spirals at the corners of your notebook. These spirals are quintessential doodles - repetitive, almost meditative patterns that emerge as your mind wanders.

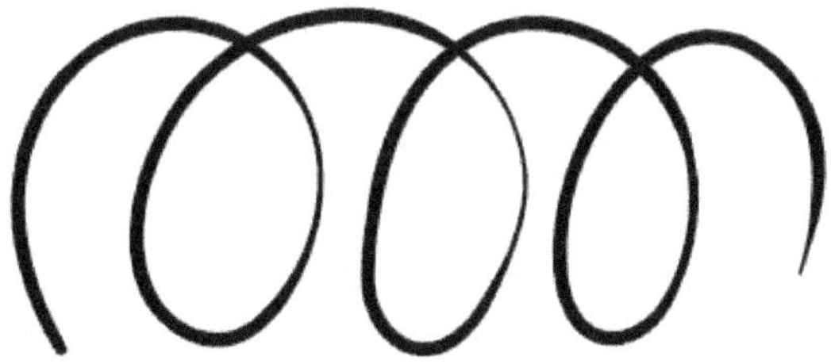

Example 2: Creative Doodling: Imagine being on hold during a phone call. As you wait, you start doodling interconnected shapes and lines, letting your hand guide the pen. The result

is an abstract pattern that wasn't pre-planned but emerged organically.

Unleashing Unconscious Expression

Doodling, unlike structured writing, taps into your unconscious mind. It's like a conversation between your hand and your inner thoughts, with the pen as the mediator. This makes doodles an authentic reflection of your inner world.

Example 1: Emotion on Paper: On a particularly stressful day, you might find yourself doodling jagged lines and sharp angles. These shapes mirror your emotional state, conveying tension and unease without you needing to explicitly describe it.

Example 2: Repetition and Rhythm: Repetitive doodles, such as rows of dots or waves of lines, provide a rhythmic outlet.

The soothing motion of creating these patterns can serve as a form of stress relief and reflection.

Doodles are a form of self-expression that bridges the gap between conscious and unconscious thought. They're like a snapshot of your inner dialogue, captured in visual form. While they may appear simple, their significance goes far beyond their appearance. So, the next time you find yourself mindlessly creating lines and shapes on paper, remember that you're engaging in a form of communication that speaks directly from your unconscious mind. It's a glimpse into your thoughts and feelings, rendered in a language that doesn't require translation.

WHEN AND WHY

Have you ever found yourself absentmindedly scribbling on a piece of paper while waiting for a call, stuck in a meeting, or simply passing time? These moments of doodling hold a secret language of their own - a language that speaks to boredom, anticipation, and even the ebb and flow of conversation

Unable to Proceed with a Task

When faced with a task that's mentally demanding or seems overwhelming, doodles can make an unexpected appearance. It's as if your brain needs a momentary escape from the challenge.

Example: Complicated Decision-Making: Imagine you're working on a complex budget spreadsheet, trying to make sense of numbers and figures. In moments of mental fatigue, you might find yourself doodling squiggly lines or random shapes, providing a brief respite from the cognitive strain.

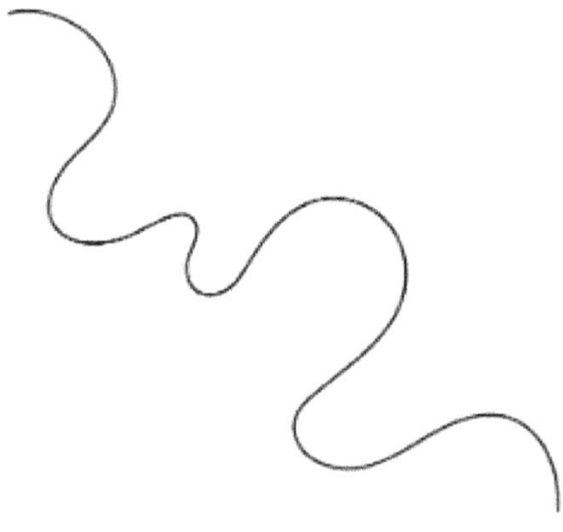

Boredom as a Catalyst

Boredom can be a fertile ground for doodles to sprout. When the mind isn't fully engaged, it seeks a simple and often subconscious outlet, leading to the creation of doodles.

Example: Mundane Meetings: Sitting through a lengthy meeting that isn't holding your attention might trigger doodles. These doodles can range from loops to intricate patterns, as your mind finds a creative diversion from the monotony.

Waiting for Something or Someone

Moments of waiting, whether for an appointment, a friend, or an event, often create an environment where doodles flourish. It's almost like your hand wants to be productive while your mind counts down the seconds.

Example: Waiting for a Flight: Sitting at the gate before a flight takes off, you might find yourself sketching small geometric shapes or repeating patterns. These doodles give you something to focus on during the anticipation.

Talking on the Phone

Doodling can be a way to occupy your hands while your attention is divided during a phone conversation. It's a form of multitasking that keeps your hand busy while your ears are engaged.

Example: Phone Conversations at Work: While on a call that doesn't require note-taking, you might find yourself doodling concentric circles or simple lines. This physical activity complements the cognitive engagement of the conversation.

So, the next time you catch yourself doodling, remember that you're engaging in an unspoken dialogue with your own mind, capturing the essence of the moment in lines and shapes on paper.

WHERE

Doodles have an uncanny ability to emerge in unexpected places, transforming any blank surface into a playground of creativity. Whether it's a scrap of paper, a corner of a magazine, or even the margins of a newspaper, doodles find their way into various nooks of our lives.

Anywhere and Everywhere

The beauty of doodling lies in its spontaneity. It can happen anywhere, be it at home, work, or while waiting in a queue. Doodling doesn't demand a designated space; it thrives on opportunity.

Example: Doodling at Home: Sitting at the kitchen table, you might grab a napkin and doodle while waiting for your tea to brew. These impromptu doodles become a testament to creativity without constraints.

A Piece of Paper

A blank piece of paper is like an open invitation for doodles. Its simplicity provides a perfect canvas for the mind to wander and express itself.

Example: Blank Notebook Pages: Opening a new notebook, you might find yourself doodling absentmindedly as you ponder ideas for your next journal entry. These doodles become a bridge between your thoughts and the written word.

Magazines and Newspapers

Even printed materials aren't safe from doodles. Magazines and newspapers become an unexpected medium for creative expression, turning mundane pages into interactive landscapes.

Example: Margin Masterpieces: Flipping through a magazine, you might discover a doodle in the margins - a playful smiley face or a trail of dots following an article. These doodles add a personal touch to the content.

Changing Faces

Doodles have a way of transforming faces, turning them into characters, emotions, or even abstract representations. Whether it's a photograph or a drawing, faces become a unique canvas for doodle expression.

Example: Expressive Eyes: Looking at a photograph of a person, you might find yourself enhancing the eyes with added lines and shading, making them appear more expressive and lifelike.

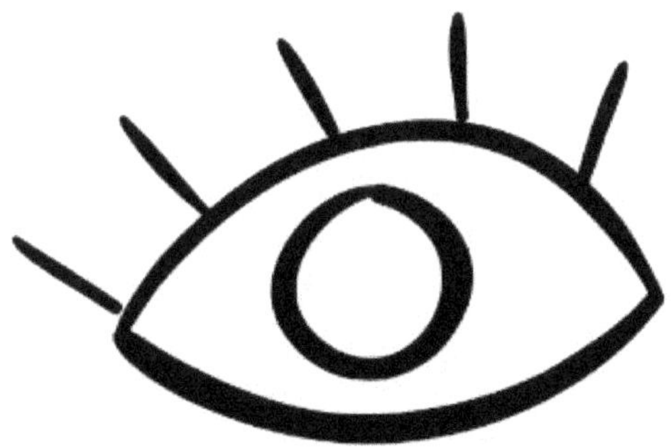

Doodles are the silent storytellers that inhabit the spaces around us. They're an organic response to a blank canvas, an instinctive way to engage with the world through marks and lines. Recognizing the diverse places where doodles emerge allows you to not only embrace the creative process but also uncover hidden corners of your thoughts and emotions. So, whether it's a slip of paper, a magazine, or even the edges of a newspaper, remember that wherever doodles find a home, they also find a way to communicate and connect with the intricacies of your inner world.

TYPES

Doodles are not just limited to simple scribbles; they encompass a vast range of expressions that go beyond mere lines on paper. These expressions include colors, shading, lines, drawings, and patterns. Each type of doodle is like a distinct instrument in the orchestra of creativity, allowing you to communicate and explore your thoughts and emotions in unique ways.

Colors: Adding colors to doodles elevates them from black and white to vibrant expressions of emotion and imagination. Colors can convey moods, emphasize elements, and create visually striking designs.
Example: Rainbow of Emotions: Imagine doodling a heart with a spectrum of colors. The colors you choose might reflect the emotions you're experiencing at that moment - red for passion, blue for tranquility, and yellow for joy.

Shading: Shading adds depth and dimension to doodles, transforming flat shapes into three-dimensional forms. It's a technique that can evoke emotions and create a sense of realism.

Example: Shaded Flower: Doodling a flower and shading the petals can bring it to life. The shading adds a sense of volume and texture, turning a simple doodle into a captivating illustration.

Lines: Lines are the building blocks of doodles, allowing you to create intricate patterns, shapes, and even convey movement. The type of lines you use can convey different emotions and ideas.

Example: Controlled Chaos: Doodling a chaotic tangle of lines might symbolize the busyness and chaos of your day. On the other hand, straight and organized lines might reflect a desire for order and structure.

Drawings: Doodles can evolve into detailed drawings that go beyond abstract shapes. Drawings allow you to capture objects, scenes, and characters, giving life to your imagination.

Example: Nature's Sketchbook: Doodling a detailed tree with leaves, branches, and roots turns it into a small piece of art. This doodle captures the essence of nature in a compact form.

Patterns: Patterns are like the language of repetition in doodles. Creating patterns can be soothing and meditative, and they can also convey a sense of rhythm and harmony.
Example: Mandala Magic: Doodling a mandala with intricate patterns radiating from the center can be a calming exercise. The repetitive nature of the patterns guides your focus and relieves stress.

POSITION

LEFT OF PAGE

The positioning of doodles on a page is like a hidden code, revealing insights into a person's personality, emotions, and experiences. When doodles are placed on the left side of the page, they offer a glimpse into the individual's inner world, social interactions, and past memories.

Left of the Page Doodles: A Window to the Inner Self
Doodles placed on the left side of a page often signify traits and tendencies related to introversion, caution, and a strong connection to the past. These doodles can reveal how a person processes emotions, relationships, and experiences.

Inner Reserve and Introversion: Doodling on the left side of the page suggests a preference for inner reflection and introspection. The person may be more reserved and contemplative, finding solace in their own thoughts.

Cautious Approach to Social Interactions: Left-side doodles can indicate a cautious approach to forming new friendships. The person may take their time to build connections and may be selective about who they allow into their inner circle.

Emphasis on Past Incidences and People: Doodles on the left side can highlight a person's strong attachment to past memories and experiences. The person may find it challenging to let go of the past and might frequently reminisce about significant moments and people.

Difficulty in Moving On: Doodles on the left side might suggest a struggle with letting go of past incidents, whether positive or negative. The person might find it challenging to forget and move forward.

The placement of doodles on the left side of a page provides a unique window into an individual's psyche. It speaks of their inner world, their approach to relationships, and their connection to the past. By understanding this placement, you can gain insights into your own thought processes and emotions, as well as those of others. So, the next time you find yourself doodling on the left side of a page, remember that you're leaving traces of your innermost thoughts and feelings, capturing a snapshot of your unique personality and experiences.

RIGHT OF THE PAGE

The position of doodles on a page unveils a hidden language that speaks volumes about a person's nature, aspirations, and social inclinations. Doodles placed on the right side of the page provide a fascinating glimpse into a person's extroverted tendencies, forward-looking mindset, and affinity for social interactions.

Right of the Page Doodles: A Glimpse into a Socially-Oriented Future

When doodles grace the right side of a page, they often signify characteristics associated with extroversion, an optimistic outlook, and a preference for the company of others. These doodles can shed light on how a person approaches life, relationships, and the future.

Outgoing and Sociable Character: Doodling on the right side of the page suggests a natural affinity for social interactions and a desire to connect with others. The person may feel energized and fulfilled through social engagement.

A Forward-Looking Mindset: Doodles on the right side indicate an inclination towards looking ahead and embracing the future with enthusiasm. The person might be drawn to new opportunities and experiences that lie ahead.

Thriving in Social Company: Doodles on the right side suggest that the person derives energy and happiness from being around others. They might find comfort in group settings and feel a sense of fulfillment through interactions.

Minimal Attachment to the Past: Doodles on the right side may indicate that the person places less emphasis on the past and is more focused on the present and future. They might not dwell on memories as much as they anticipate upcoming experiences.

The placement of doodles on the right side of a page unveils a person's dynamic, forward-looking, and socially-engaged personality. It reveals how they approach relationships, embrace new experiences, and thrive in the company of others. So, the next time your doodles find their way to the right side of the page, remember that you're leaving traces of your optimistic outlook and your eagerness to embrace the possibilities that lie ahead.

CENTER OF THE PAGE

The placement of doodles on a page is like a silent storyteller, revealing intricate details about a person's desire for attention, their extroverted nature, and their need to stand out. When doodles claim the center of the page, they offer a fascinating glimpse into an individual's quest for recognition and their vibrant personality.

Center of the Page Doodles: A Window into a Vibrant Persona

Doodles positioned at the center of a page often convey traits linked to extroversion, a strong need for acknowledgment, and a desire to be in the limelight. These doodles shed light on how a person seeks attention, engages with others, and leaves a memorable impression.

Seeking Attention and Recognition: Doodling at the center of the page signifies a natural inclination to be noticed and acknowledged. The person might thrive on the attention they receive from others and actively seek ways to capture the spotlight.

Energetic and Engaging Persona: Centered doodles suggest a vibrant personality that draws people in. The person might be outgoing, enthusiastic, and captivating in social situations.

Making a Lasting Impression: Doodles at the center of the page can reveal a person's intent to make their presence unforgettable. They might aim to leave an indelible mark on the memories of those they interact with.
Sociable and Approachable Nature: Centered doodles might reflect a person's approachable demeanor and their ability to connect with various individuals. They might be skilled at making everyone feel included and valued.

The placement of doodles at the center of a page uncovers a person's need for attention, their engaging personality, and their drive to leave an impact. It offers insights into how they navigate social interactions, stand out in a crowd, and make their presence felt. So, the next time your doodles find their home at the center of the page, remember that you're expressing your vibrant persona and your desire to be an influential presence in the lives of those around you.

UPPER PAGE

Doodle placements on a page hold the keys to understanding an individual's idealism, optimism, and imaginative nature. When doodles grace the upper part of the page, they offer a fascinating glimpse into a person's lofty ideas, positive outlook, and creative imagination.

Upper Page Doodles: A Peek into an Imaginative Mindset
Doodles situated in the upper portion of a page often reveal characteristics tied to idealism, a sunny disposition, and a tendency to generate creative ideas. These doodles provide insight into how a person approaches challenges, sees the world, and expresses their imagination.

Idealism and Positive Outlook: Doodling at the upper part of the page suggests a naturally idealistic perspective and an optimistic outlook on life. The person might see the best in people and situations, embracing the potential for positive outcomes.

Constant Flow of Ideas: Upper page doodles can indicate a mind that's constantly buzzing with creative thoughts and ideas. The person might find joy in brainstorming and exploring innovative solutions.

Imaginative and Dreamy Nature: Doodles placed in the upper portion of the page suggest a vivid imagination and a propensity for daydreaming. The person might enjoy exploring fantastical scenarios and envisioning different possibilities.

Positive Problem-Solving Approach: Upper page doodles might reveal an individual's tendency to approach challenges with a positive and creative mindset. They might view difficulties as opportunities for growth and transformation.

The placement of doodles in the upper part of a page offers a window into a person's idealistic outlook, creative spark, and imaginative tendencies. It provides insights into how they approach problem-solving, interact with their environment, and infuse their life with positivity. So, the next time your doodles find their way to the upper part of the page, remember that you're leaving traces of your imaginative spirit and your optimistic approach to life's adventures.

LOWER PAGE

The placement of doodles on a page holds the key to understanding an individual's self-promotion tendencies, emotional nuances, and inner compulsions. When doodles find their place at the lower part of the page, they unveil insights into a person's reserved nature, reluctance to self-promote, and the emotional depths they might be navigating.

Lower Page Doodles: Unveiling the Inner Landscape
Doodles positioned in the lower part of a page often reveal traits tied to introversion, a hesitancy to seek attention, and potential emotional undercurrents. These doodles provide a window into how a person interacts with the world, expresses themselves, and processes their emotions.

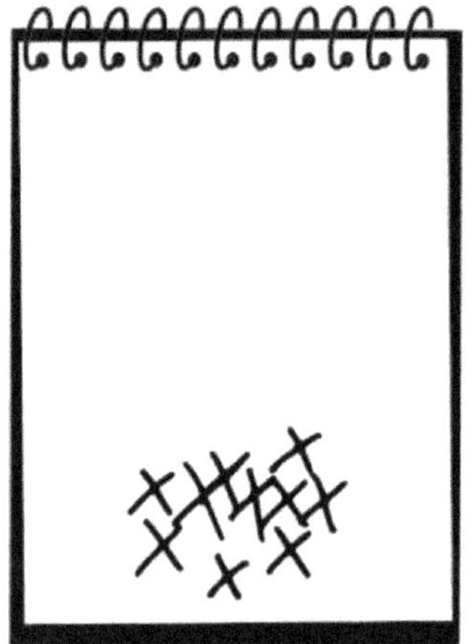

Reserved and Less Extroverted Nature: Doodling at the lower part of the page suggests a more introverted disposition and a preference for keeping a lower profile. The person might be more comfortable in smaller, intimate settings rather than seeking out the spotlight.

Reluctance to Self-Promote: Lower page doodles can indicate a reluctance to draw attention to oneself or engage in self-promotion. The person might downplay their achievements and prefer to let their work speak for itself.

Emotional and Mental Compulsions: Doodles placed in the lower portion of the page might be linked to emotional or mental compulsions. They can offer insight into the person's internal struggles or the need to process emotions in a more private manner.

Expression of Vulnerability: Lower page doodles might reveal an individual's willingness to express vulnerability and reveal their inner thoughts and emotions. They might use doodles as a way to share their personal narrative.

The placement of doodles in the lower part of a page provides insights into an individual's introverted tendencies, emotional expressions, and their unique way of navigating self-expression. It allows you to recognize your own inclination towards quiet introspection and thoughtful expression, as well as to understand these traits in others. So, the next time your doodles find their place at the lower edge of the page, remember that you're leaving traces of your introspective nature and your ability to process emotions in your own meaningful way.

PRESSURE

HEAVY

The pressure with which doodles are created on a page can offer a profound glimpse into an individual's emotional state, responses to stress, and potential displays of temper. When doodles are marked by heavy pressure, they reveal insights into how a person reacts to their moods, handles stress, and expresses their emotions.

Heavy Pressure Doodles: Unveiling Emotional Response
Doodles created with heavy pressure often reflect an individual's immediate emotional state and their response to stress. The way they apply pressure to the pen or pencil can convey their emotional intensity, demonstrating their capacity for aggression or temper display.

Reflecting the Mood of the Moment: Doodles marked with heavy pressure indicate that the person is strongly influenced by their immediate emotions and current mood. Their doodles serve as a visual representation of their feelings at that precise moment.

Elements of Stress and Aggression: Heavy pressure doodles can signify a degree of stress and even aggression. The person might channel their emotional intensity into their doodles, using them as a safe outlet to release pent-up feelings.

Display of Temper and Intensity: Doodles marked with heavy pressure might also indicate an outright display of temper or intensity. The person might use their doodles as a means to express their frustrations or anger.

Emotional Catharsis: Heavy pressure doodles can serve as a form of emotional catharsis, allowing the person to release their emotional tension in a tangible and expressive manner.

The pressure with which doodles are created on a page offers a window into an individual's immediate emotional responses, stress coping mechanisms, and the potential for displaying temper. It enables you to understand your own emotional expressiveness and stress management techniques, as well as recognize these traits in others. So, the next time your doodles are marked with heavy pressure, remember that you're capturing the intensity of your emotions in that moment and using your creative expression as a powerful tool for emotional release and self-awareness.

MEDIUM

The pressure applied to create doodles on a page can provide a significant glimpse into an individual's emotional equilibrium, mood, and potential underlying discrepancies. When doodles are marked with medium pressure, they offer insights into a person's balanced mood and emotional state, while also prompting us to examine the subject matter for any hidden inconsistencies.

Medium Pressure Doodles: Balancing Emotions and Subjects

Doodles crafted with medium pressure often mirror an individual's well-balanced emotional state and mood. The pressure level used signifies a healthy equilibrium, but it's essential to also scrutinize the subject matter of the doodles for potential inconsistencies.

Balanced and Reasonable Mood: Doodles marked with medium pressure suggest that the person is experiencing a balanced and reasonable emotional state. Their doodles reflect a state of equilibrium, where emotions are neither overly intense nor suppressed.

Checking for Discrepancies in Mood: While medium pressure doodles indicate a balanced mood, it's crucial to analyze the subject matter of the doodles. Discrepancies between the pressure and the emotional theme of the doodles might indicate underlying emotional nuances.

Expressing Emotional Harmony: Medium pressure doodles reflect a person's ability to express their emotions in a harmonious and balanced manner. They might be comfortable sharing their feelings openly, yet maintaining a sense of emotional stability.

Recognizing Emotional Health: Medium pressure doodles can signify a healthy approach to emotions, where feelings are acknowledged and expressed without overwhelming intensity. The individual might have cultivated emotional intelligence and self-awareness.

The pressure applied to doodles on a page provides insights into an individual's emotional balance and the way they express their feelings. It's an invitation to examine the content of the doodles and explore potential hidden emotions or discrepancies. So, the next time you find yourself creating medium pressure doodles, remember that you're showcasing your ability to harmoniously express your emotions and thoughts through your creative expression.

LIGHT

The pressure applied while creating doodles offers a fascinating insight into an individual's receptivity, sensitivity, and potential for being influenced. When doodles are marked with light pressure, they unveil traits of a person who is receptive to their surroundings and easily influenced by external factors.

Light Pressure Doodles: Revealing Receptivity and Sensitivity

Doodles crafted with light pressure provide a window into an individual's receptive nature and sensitivity. The gentle touch with which they create their doodles suggests a propensity for being influenced by their environment and external stimuli.

Receptive and Open-Minded Nature: Doodles marked with light pressure signify that the person possesses a receptive and open-minded disposition. They are likely to be attuned to the world around them and willing to embrace new ideas and experiences.

Sensitivity to Surroundings: Light pressure doodles often reveal an individual's sensitivity to their surroundings. Their creations reflect their capacity to pick up on subtle nuances in their environment and respond to them creatively.

Easiness of Influence: Doodles marked with light pressure suggest that the person is easily influenced by external factors, whether it's the emotions of others, prevailing trends, or the mood of the environment.

Reflecting Emotional Resonance: Light pressure doodles often mirror an individual's emotional resonance with their subject matter. Their gentle strokes indicate a connection between their feelings and the creative process.

The pressure applied to doodles on a page provides insights into an individual's receptivity, sensitivity, and capacity for being influenced by their surroundings. It invites you to recognize your own open-mindedness, emotional connection with your surroundings, and the ease with which you absorb external influences. So, the next time you find yourself creating light pressure doodles, remember that you're showcasing your receptivity to the world around you and your ability to translate your sensitivity into meaningful art.

VARIABLE

The pressure applied while doodling offers a unique insight into an individual's emotional stability and reliability. When doodles are marked with variable pressure, they unveil traits of someone who experiences emotional instability, swinging between high and low moments. This can also reflect unreliability in their actions and responses.

Variable Pressure Doodles: Reflecting Emotional Swings and Unreliability
Doodles created with variable pressure provide a glimpse into an individual's emotional fluctuations and potential unreliability. The changing pressure levels mirror their shifting emotional states, contributing to their varying responses and behaviors.

Emotional Instability: Doodles marked with variable pressure indicate that the person experiences emotional instability. Their creations may reflect rapid shifts between different emotional states, impacting their mood and interactions.

Fluctuating Responses: Variable pressure doodles often mirror an individual's fluctuating responses to situations and interactions. Their emotional swings can lead to unpredictable reactions, making them appear inconsistent in their behavior.

Unreliable Behavior: Doodles marked with variable pressure can reflect a degree of unreliability in an individual's actions and decisions. Their emotional fluctuations might impact their commitment to plans and consistency in their interactions.

Creative Exploration: Variable pressure doodles can also indicate an individual's inclination for creative exploration. The changing pressure levels might reflect their willingness to experiment with different techniques and styles.

The pressure applied to doodles on a page provides insights into an individual's emotional stability and reliability. It invites you to recognize your own emotional fluctuations and their impact on your actions and responses. So, the next time you find yourself creating variable pressure doodles, remember that you're capturing the ebb and flow of your emotions and uncovering insights into your own reliability and responsiveness.

TYPES

SHADING

The shading technique employed in doodles offers a unique window into an individual's emotional state and thought patterns. When doodles incorporate shading, they often reveal underlying anxiety and the presence of negative thinking patterns. These shaded drawings can signify that the doodler might be grappling with challenges and finding it difficult to navigate their problems.

Shaded Doodles: Unveiling Anxiety and Negative Patterns
Doodles created with shading provide valuable insights into an individual's emotional landscape, indicating their struggles with anxiety and negative thought patterns. The presence of shading suggests a level of complexity and depth to their emotional experiences.

Implication of Anxiety: Shaded doodles often imply that the person is dealing with underlying anxiety. The shading technique can symbolize the layers of worry and unease that cloud their thoughts and emotions.

Negative Thinking Patterns: Shaded doodles can also reveal negative thinking patterns that the person might be trapped in. The shading adds a dimension of intensity, reflecting their tendency to focus on problems and difficulties.

Complexity of Emotions: Shading in doodles signifies the complexity of emotions experienced by the individual. The shades and tones added to the drawings convey the layers of feelings they're navigating.

Challenges in Finding Solutions: Shaded doodles suggest that the person might be struggling to find clear solutions to their problems. The shading might reflect their difficulty in seeing a way out of their challenges.

The shading technique used in doodles provides insights into an individual's emotional struggles, anxiety, and negative thinking patterns. It encourages you to recognize your own emotional complexity and the impact of shading on the overall mood of your doodles. So, the next time you find yourself incorporating shading into your doodles, remember that you're shedding light on your inner emotions and thought processes, and it's an opportunity to address and work through any challenges you may be facing.

CURVED LINES

The use of curved and wavy lines in doodles offers a unique glimpse into an individual's emotional reactions and perceptions of their surroundings. When doodles incorporate these types of lines, they often reveal an emotional response to the doodler's interpretation of events. These lines can signify an emotional connection between the doodler's thoughts and their perception of reality.

Curved and Wavy Lines in Doodles: Expressing Emotional Responses
Doodles created with curved and wavy lines provide a valuable window into an individual's emotional landscape, indicating their emotional reactions to their perceptions of reality.

Emotional Connection: Curved lines in doodles imply an emotional connection between the doodler's thoughts and their interpretation of events. The fluidity of the lines reflects the emotional energy invested in the doodle.

Reflecting Mood and Perception: Curved and wavy lines in doodles mirror the doodler's mood and perception of their environment. The variations in the lines convey a sense of movement and emotional flow.

Emotional Reactions to Events: Curved lines in doodles often signify emotional reactions to events or situations. The curves capture the doodler's interpretation of events and the emotional impact they have.

Symbolism of Flow and Movement: Curved and wavy lines can symbolize the flow and movement of emotions within the doodler. The lines suggest the ebb and flow of feelings and thoughts.

The use of curved and wavy lines in doodles provides insights into an individual's emotional reactions and their interpretation of events. It encourages you to recognize your own emotional connections to your thoughts and perceptions, as well as the fluidity of your emotions. So, the next time you find yourself incorporating curved and wavy lines into your doodles, remember that you're capturing the emotional flow of your thoughts and reactions, and it's an opportunity to explore your own emotional landscape.

STRAIGHT LINES

The presence of straight lines in doodles offers a unique insight into an individual's emotional traits, including their constructiveness, determination, and even a touch of aggression. When doodles incorporate straight lines, they often reveal the doodler's approach to challenges, goals, and their emotional disposition. These lines can signify a strong sense of purpose and a particular emotional energy within the doodler.

Straight Lines in Doodles: Unveiling Emotional Traits and Determination

Doodles created with straight lines provide valuable clues about an individual's emotional disposition, reflecting their approach to various situations and challenges.

Constructiveness and Determination: Straight lines in doodles often signify a constructive and determined approach to life. These lines suggest a purposeful and focused mindset, driven by clear goals and objectives.

Symbolism of Order and Control: The presence of straight lines indicates a desire for order and control. These lines reflect the doodler's inclination to create structure and organization in their life.

Hint of Aggression and Assertiveness: Straight lines in doodles can also reveal a touch of aggression and assertiveness in the doodler's emotional disposition. These lines suggest a drive to take charge and assert themselves.

Linear Approach to Problem-Solving: The use of straight lines indicates a linear and logical approach to problem-solving. The doodler might prefer tackling challenges methodically and step by step.

The presence of straight lines in doodles provides insights into an individual's emotional traits, including their constructiveness, determination, and assertiveness. It encourages you to recognize your own approach to challenges, goals, and your emotional disposition. So, the next time you find yourself incorporating straight lines into your doodles, remember that you're expressing your determination and emotional traits, and it's an opportunity to channel these energies into your pursuits and aspirations.

UNDERLINES

The presence of underlines in doodles offers a fascinating insight into an individual's emotional defensiveness and their relationship with authority figures. Underlines in doodles often symbolize the creation of a protective platform, a stance taken to safeguard oneself emotionally. These lines can reveal an individual's need for a strong foundation in the face of challenges and interactions with authority.

Underlines in Doodles: Reflecting Emotional Defensiveness and Authority Dynamics

Doodles featuring underlines provide valuable clues about an individual's emotional defensiveness and their response to authority figures or challenging situations.

Emotional Defensiveness: Underlines in doodles often signify emotional defensiveness, creating a metaphorical barrier to protect the doodler's thoughts and emotions. It suggests a need to establish a foundation of protection.

Creating a Platform for Communication: Underlines in doodles can also represent the creation of a platform for communication. It implies a desire to be heard and understood, establishing a base upon which to convey thoughts and opinions.

Authority Dynamics: Underlines in doodles can reflect an individual's response to authority figures. If the underline is present at the top of the doodle, it might symbolize protection from those in positions of authority.

Establishing Boundaries: Underlines can also indicate a desire to set emotional boundaries in relationships or interactions. It suggests creating a clear demarcation between oneself and external influences.

The presence of underlines in doodles provides insights into an individual's emotional defensiveness and their dynamics with authority figures. It encourages you to recognize your own need for emotional protection, your desire to communicate clearly, and your response to authority in various situations. So, the next time you find yourself incorporating underlines into your doodles, remember that you're expressing your need for emotional protection and creating a platform for communication, all while managing your response to authority dynamics.

REPETITION

The presence of repetition in doodles offers intriguing insights into an individual's emotional traits, including impulsiveness, discontent, and even possible signs of obsessive behavior. Repetition in doodle patterns can reveal the doodler's emotional responses, their level of patience, and their approach to handling challenging emotions.

Repetition in Doodles: Unveiling Impulsiveness, Discontent, and Obsessive Behavior
Patterns featuring repetition in doodles provide valuable clues about an individual's emotional reactions and their tendencies when confronted with different situations.

Impulsiveness and Irritation: Repetition in doodles often signifies an impulsive nature, reflecting a tendency to speak one's mind without hesitation. It can also indicate a heightened level of irritability, where the individual reacts quickly to stimuli.

Discontent and Emotional Tensions: Patterns with repetition can also suggest discontent and emotional tensions within the doodler. The repetitive nature might be a reflection of internal conflicts or dissatisfaction.

Possible Obsessive Behavior: Repetition in doodles can sometimes hint at obsessive behavior. The continuous repetition might reveal a preoccupation with a specific thought or idea.

Coping Mechanism for Stress: Repetition in doodles can serve as a coping mechanism for stress. Creating repetitive patterns might help individuals manage their emotions and find a sense of relief.

The presence of repetition in doodles provides insights into an individual's emotional traits, including impulsiveness, discontent, and potential signs of obsessive behavior. It encourages you to recognize your own impulsive tendencies, emotional tensions, and the coping mechanisms you employ when faced with challenges. So, the next time you find yourself incorporating repetition into your doodles, remember that you're expressing various emotional responses, and it's an opportunity to explore your impulses, emotions, and coping mechanisms more deeply.

COLOURS

RED

Colors in doodles hold deeper meanings that can provide insights into an individual's emotions, thoughts, and even subconscious desires. The color red, in particular, signifies energy and sexuality, reflecting a range of emotions and characteristics

The Color Red: Symbolizing Energy and Sexuality
When you use red in your doodles, you're tapping into a color that carries powerful connotations related to energy, passion, and sexuality.

Red is often associated with vitality, strength, and high energy levels. Red is the color of passion and intense emotions. Red is also closely associated with sensuality and sexuality. Red is a bold and attention-grabbing color. Red is often associated with warning signs and signals caution.

BROWN

Colors in doodles carry profound meanings that can offer insights into an individual's emotions, thoughts, and even subconscious concerns. Brown, a color often associated with earthiness, can reveal insights into personal security and common sense.

The Color Brown: Symbolizing Personal Security and Common Sense
When you incorporate brown into your doodles, you're tapping into a color that holds implications related to personal security and practicality.

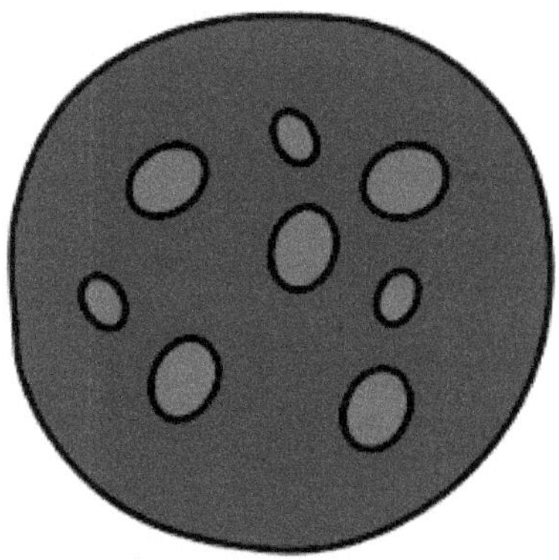

Brown is often linked to the earth and nature, symbolizing stability and grounding. Brown is associated with practicality, reliability, and common sense. Brown is often seen as a warm and comforting color. Brown is strongly associated with nature, earth, and the environment. Brown can reflect your pragmatic thinking and rational decision-making.

GREY

Colors within doodles hold the power to reveal deep-seated emotions, thoughts, and psychological states. Grey, often associated with neutrality and subtlety, can signify feelings of depression, defeat, and the role of a neutral observer.

The Color Grey: Uncovering Depression, Defeat, and Neutral Observation
When grey makes an appearance in doodles, it serves as a visual gateway to the emotions and perspectives of the creator.

Grey is often associated with feelings of sadness, depression, and defeat. Grey serves as a neutral color, suggesting impartiality and detachment. Grey is often seen as a subtle and complex color, representing nuances that might not be immediately evident. Grey can symbolize a desire for balance and composure. Grey often exists between black and white, representing transitions and adaptations.

BLACK

Colors within doodles hold a remarkable ability to unveil hidden emotions, thoughts, and psychological states. Black, a color often associated with depth and intensity, can signify feelings of anxiety, irritability, and the desire for clear communication.

The Color Black: Unveiling Anxiety, Irritability, and Clarity
When black emerges in doodles, it serves as a visual key to the creator's emotions and intentions.

Black is often linked to feelings of anxiety, tension, and emotional heaviness. Black signifies depth and intensity, reflecting a tendency for introspection and contemplation. Black can symbolize the quest for clarity and straightforward communication. Black may also represent irritability and a sense of tension. Black can symbolize the attempt to bring order to chaos.

PINK

Colors within doodles hold the power to unravel a tapestry of emotions and psychological nuances. Pink, often associated with femininity and tenderness, can reveal insights into an individual's feminine qualities, regardless of their gender.

The Color Pink: Embracing Femininity and Sensitivity
Pink is a hue that carries connotations of gentleness, sensitivity, and the expression of emotions. When pink emerges in doodles, it serves as a visual window into the creator's emotional world.

Pink is traditionally linked to femininity, nurturing qualities, and a tender demeanor. Pink is also associated with emotional sensitivity and depth. Pink can evoke a sense of playfulness, innocence, and youthfulness. Pink can symbolize inner harmony, compassion, and the ability to connect with others on an emotional level. Pink's versatility extends beyond traditional gender associations.

BLUE

Colors within doodles have the extraordinary ability to provide glimpses into our emotions, thoughts, and psyche. Blue, a color often associated with calmness and reflection, holds the key to understanding an individual's contemplative nature.

The Color Blue: A Window into Reflective States
Blue is a color that conveys a sense of tranquility, introspection, and depth. When blue emerges in doodles, it serves as a visual representation of the creator's contemplative mind.

Blue is often associated with calmness and serenity, making it a powerful symbol of inner reflection. Blue can also signify emotional depth and the capacity to explore complex feelings. Blue's association with calmness and open space can indicate an open-minded and receptive attitude. Blue's tranquil qualities can suggest a desire for mental clarity and peace. Blue's association with the vastness of the sky and sea can symbolize a thirst for knowledge, exploration, and a broader understanding of the world.

GREEN

Colors in doodles can speak volumes about our emotions, thoughts, and subconscious desires. Among these, the color green holds a unique significance, often tied to feelings of envy or jealousy.

The Color Green: Uncovering Envy and Jealousy
Green is a color that evokes a wide range of emotions, from growth and harmony to envy and jealousy. When green emerges in doodles, it can serve as a visual indicator of the artist's emotional state, particularly in relation to envy or jealousy.

Green is often associated with envy and jealousy, emotions that can arise when one desires something possessed by another. Green's association with envy and jealousy can also symbolize the complexities of human emotions. Green can signify emotional sensitivity and a heightened awareness of interpersonal dynamics. Green's association with growth and harmony can also indicate an individual's aspiration for personal development and balance. Green's connection to nature can represent appreciation for the beauty and abundance of the natural world.

YELLOW

Colors in doodles are like windows into our thoughts and emotions. Among these, the color yellow carries significant implications, often tied to financial concerns and material matters.

The Color Yellow: A Glimpse into Financial Worries and Material Matters

Yellow is a color that resonates with a range of emotions, from optimism and clarity to caution and anxiety. When yellow appears in doodles, it can serve as a visual indicator of the artist's feelings and thoughts related to finances and material concerns.

Yellow in doodles can symbolize financial worries, indicating concerns about money, expenses, and economic stability. Yellow can also be associated with caution and careful decision-making, especially in matters related to money and material possessions. Yellow's association with clarity and rational thinking can indicate an individual's approach to financial matters with a practical mindset. Yellow's association with material possessions can indicate an individual's focus on acquiring and maintaining belongings.

PURPLE, VIOLET and LILAC

Colors in doodles offer a unique lens into an individual's inner world, revealing emotions, personality traits, and even hidden desires. Among these colors, purple, violet, and lilac hold a special place, often hinting at an individual's need for emotional consistency, sensitivity, and creative expression.

Embracing Emotional Consistency: Purple, Violet, and Lilac Doodles
The presence of purple, violet, or lilac hues in doodles can signal a range of emotions and personality characteristics

Purple, violet, and lilac are often associated with emotional depth and sensitivity. The presence of purple, violet, or lilac in doodles can also indicate an individual's desire for emotional stability and equilibrium. Purple, violet, and lilac are often associated with femininity, artistic expression, and creativity. Purple, violet, and lilac hues can also signify heightened sensory awareness and an individual's appreciation for the subtleties of the world around them. Purple, violet, and lilac are colors often associated with depth and complexity.

EMOTIONAL DOODLES

FACES

Relationship Difficulty Drama
Doodling faces may reflect recent or ongoing relationship challenges. The faces become a canvas expressing the emotional landscapes of your connections.

Happy Faces, Smooth Seas
Happy faces in your doodles signify a state of well-being. They are visual echoes of contentment and harmonious moments.

Sad or Serious Shadows
Sad or serious faces suggest difficulties rooted in a lack of cooperation with others. The gravity of the expressions mirrors a struggle with interpersonal dynamics.

Hats as Shields
When a hat covers the head or one eye, it symbolizes a self-protective streak. It may indicate a desire to shield oneself from external scrutiny or vulnerability.

Ego's Canvas
Self-portraits in doodles serve as extensions of ego. Whether complimentary or not, they reveal the artist's perception of themselves.

Beauty and Distrust

Beautiful and attractive faces convey a positive and optimistic outlook. Conversely, ugly faces represent a negative or distrustful view.

Eyes Tell Tales

Detailed eyes in doodles may suggest a desire to be noticed or a feeling of being watched. The level of intricacy mirrors the intensity of these emotions.

Voluptuous Lips, Secret Desires

Lush, voluptuous lips in doodles may signify deep-seated, secret desires. The sensuality of the lips becomes a metaphor for hidden longings.

Face Directional Dialogue

The direction of the face in doodles speaks volumes. Left-facing indicates a gaze into the past, while right-facing signifies a focus on the future.

ANIMALS

Fondness for Furry Friends

Doodling animals implies a general fondness for them. It may suggest a desire to have a pet or reflect aspects of your personality related to the nature of the animal.

Elephant Weight

An elephant in your doodles may symbolize a weight problem or a sense of heaviness in your life. It serves as a visual metaphor for challenges that feel substantial.

Bull or Lion Leadership

Doodling a bull or lion signifies leadership qualities, a desire to dominate, conquer, and a sense of superiority over others.

Monkey or Parrot Humor

Doodling a monkey or parrot suggests a sense of humor. These playful creatures symbolize lightheartedness and the ability to find joy in various situations.

Tiger or Wolf Unexpressed Anger

A doodle of a tiger or wolf may reveal hidden, unexpressed anger. These powerful creatures represent emotions lurking beneath the surface.

Sly Fox Intentions

A doodled fox suggests a desire to do something sly or cunning. It may point to strategic thinking or a playful inclination toward cleverness.

Squirrel Care and Protection

Drawing a squirrel indicates a need for care and protection. The doodle reflects a subconscious desire for nurturance and support.

Repeated Animal Comparisons

Doodling the same animal repeatedly suggests an unconscious comparison to that animal's character. It implies an attempt to emulate certain qualities.

BOXES AND CUBES

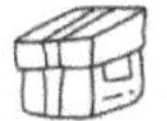 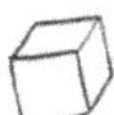    

Spontaneous Expression

If you find yourself doodling boxes in meetings, it indicates a spontaneous need to comment or express thoughts. Your attention is easily aroused, prompting you to engage verbally.

Controlled and Ambitious Nature

Boxes signify a controlled and controlling nature. Precision, logic, and practicality are prominent traits. The doodles also hint at materialism and ambition.

Emotional Attention to Detail

Shaded boxes reveal an emotional approach and extra attention to detail. The shading adds a layer of emotional depth to your logical thinking.

Efficient and Analytical Control

Cubes in doodles indicate an efficient, analytical, and in-control personality. It suggests a logical approach to problem-solving and a structured mindset.

Logical Problem-Solving

Doodling cubes when facing unsolved problems suggests a logical approach to working through challenges. It reflects a step-by-step methodical thinking process.

Overwhelmed Pile or Stack

Beware if your boxes form a pile or stack, as it may indicate feelings of overwhelm. The visual representation mirrors the emotional load you might be experiencing.

Love for Order and Planning

Symmetrical shapes within boxes reveal a love of order and a disposition to thoroughly plan and calculate. It signifies a clear vision of goals and a commitment to personal opinions.

CHECKERBOARD

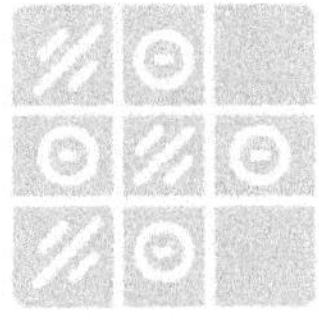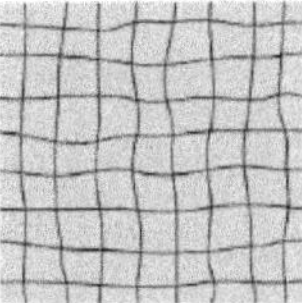

Checkerboard doodles provide a fascinating window into your thoughts and emotions, offering insights into your problem-solving approach, patience, and the complexities you might be grappling with in your life.

Logical Problem-Solving
The checkerboard pattern signifies a methodical and logical approach to problem-solving. Each square represents a considered decision or step taken in the intricate game of life. If you find checkerboards frequenting your doodles, it indicates an ongoing process of working through challenges with a clear and structured mindset.

Patience and Persistence
The checkerboard suggests a patient and persistent nature. Much like playing a game of checkers, you approach challenges with the understanding that not every move leads to an immediate solution. Instead, your doodles reflect a commitment to enduring the journey and patiently considering each move.

Unpleasant Situations and Inner Conflict

If checkerboards persistently appear in your doodles, it might be an indication of current discomfort or inner conflict. The repetitive nature of the pattern could highlight unresolved issues or doubts about the path you're on. The squares might represent aspects of your life that feel conflicting or challenging.

Quest for Self-Discovery

Checkerboard patterns can also signify a quest for self-discovery and a search for life's mission. The ordered arrangement of squares may represent the various possibilities and choices in your life, prompting introspection and a desire for clarity.

Hidden Issues and Inner Reflection

Persistent checkerboard doodles could be a subconscious expression of hidden concerns or issues that you may not be fully aware of. The regular appearance of this pattern suggests a need for introspection to uncover and address these underlying challenges.

TREES

Optimistic Aspirations

Trees with leaves or branches pointing upward indicate an optimistic personality. It symbolizes a person with positive aspirations and a hopeful outlook.

Deeper Shadows of Depression

When tree branches or leaves point downward, it may suggest feelings of depression. The downward orientation reflects inner emotions of sadness or melancholy.

Warm-Hearted Sociability

A well-rounded tree in your doodle signifies a pleasant, sociable nature. It represents someone who is warm-hearted, friendly, and enjoys social interactions.

Touchy Personality Traits

Pointed or hard-angled versions of trees suggest a touchy personality. It hints at someone who may be sensitive or easily affected by external factors.

Sarcastic Under Pressure

A Christmas tree doodle, typically pointed, indicates a sarcastic nature. Under pressure, this person may become aggressive, using sarcasm as a defense mechanism.

Anxiety and Unrealistic Thinking

Drawing the ground around the base of the tree may signify anxiety and reservation of unrealistic thinking. It reflects a mind grappling with uncertainties.

Solitary Reflection or Phallic Symbolism

A lone tree in a doodle could represent solitary reflection or even carry phallic symbolism, indicating personal introspection or desires.

Forest of Thoughts

A group of trees suggests developing thoughts. It represents a mind teeming with ideas, experiences, and a rich landscape of evolving perspectives.

HEARTS

Emotional Vulnerability

When hearts appear in your doodles, it's a visual expression of emotional vulnerability. This often occurs after a relationship has ended, signifying the emotional impact of the breakup.

Quantifying Emotion

The number of heart shapes in your doodles correlates with the intensity of your emotions. More hearts suggest a heightened emotional state, reflecting the depth of your feelings.

Nested Hearts

If you draw hearts within each other, it indicates a desire for more affection. This nested arrangement symbolizes a need for deeper connections and a longing for increased emotional warmth.

Heartbreak Patterns

Drawing hearts in patterns might signify a repetitive emotional theme, specifically related to heartbreak or unresolved emotions. The pattern reflects a recurring emotional experience.

Inverted Hearts

Inverting hearts, drawing them upside down, can symbolize a sense of emotional upheaval. It may represent feelings of confusion, sadness, or a shift in emotional balance.

Heart Density

The density of hearts in a specific area of your doodle can highlight a focal point of emotional significance. A concentrated cluster of hearts may point to a specific emotional issue or memory.

Symbolic Coloration

The color you use for hearts can add layers of meaning. For instance, red may signify passion or intense emotions, while softer colors might represent gentler or more subdued feelings.

Heart Trails

Drawing hearts in a trail-like pattern suggests a journey through emotions. It signifies the progression or movement of your feelings over time.

WAVES

Garlanded Waves
If your waves take on a garlanded appearance, it reflects an open and friendly nature. This suggests a person who is approachable and enjoys building connections with others.

Arcade Waves
Arcade-shaped waves indicate a secretive nature. The doodler may possess the ability to conceal their intentions or thoughts, creating a sense of mystery around them.

Objects or People in the Water
If your doodle includes objects or people in the water, it might represent the source of a subconscious problem or contemplation. The items submerged signify elements that are influencing your thoughts.

Underwater Scenes
If your waves depict an underwater scene, it suggests a lack of clarity or visibility regarding a specific issue. The doodler is unable to see a clear answer or resolution at the moment of creating the doodle.

Emotional Flux
The overall flow and pattern of the waves can symbolize the emotional flux you're experiencing. Calm, rhythmic waves might indicate emotional stability, while turbulent or erratic waves may suggest inner turmoil.

Contemplative Waves

Doodling waves may be a form of contemplation. The act of drawing them allows you to process and explore your emotions, providing a creative outlet for introspection.

Symbolic Coloration

The color you use for waves can add another layer of meaning. Calm, cool colors might represent a serene emotional state, while bold or dark colors may signify intensity or depth.

The Language of Motion

The motion of the waves - whether gentle or turbulent - speaks to the dynamics of your emotions. The doodle captures a snapshot of your emotional state in that particular moment.

FLOWERS

Circular Flowers with Rounded Petals
The more circular and rounded the flower, the more amicable the drawer is. This doodle signifies a positive and friendly disposition.

Circular Flower with Linked Stem
A circular flower with a linked stem symbolizes the womb. This might signify a connection to fertility, motherhood, or the nurturing aspects of your personality.

Circular Center with Pointy Leaves or Thorns
A circular center denotes a kind-hearted individual, but pointy leaves or thorns suggest defensiveness or distrust. This could be the expression of someone who, despite being kind, has faced betrayals or struggles with trust.

Perky vs. Droopy Flowers
Perky flowers indicate openness and a carefree attitude, while droopy or dying flowers suggest an unwillingness to open up. The state of the flowers reflects your emotional stance.

Pressure and Meaning
Heavy pressure in drawing flowers may carry sexual meaning, while light pressure could indicate a desire for a return to what a relationship used to mean.

Sentimental Romanticism

The flower doodler may be a sentimental romantic with a gentle, passive, and fragile nature. The doodles serve as a delicate expression of emotions susceptible to external forces.

Multiple Flowers with Petals Dropping

More than one flower, quickly drawn with some petals dropping, can be a phallic symbol. This might indicate a specific mindset or emotional state related to relationships.

Symbolic Flowers

- Rose: Symbolizes love.
- Rose with Thorns: Indicates betrayal or challenges in love.
- Dark-Colored Rose: Represents mourning.
- Lotus: Signifies spirituality.
- Lily or Tulip: Symbolizes rebirth or renewal.

BIRDS

Desire to Soar
Bird doodles often suggest a desire to fly away and leave behind the current circumstances. It symbolizes a longing for freedom and escape.

Big Birds or Birds of Prey
Larger birds or birds of prey in your doodle can imply feelings of resentment. It indicates a sense of waiting for the right moment to seek revenge.

Patience in Revenge
A doodler of this type may wait a long time to get even. The saying "revenge is best served cold" aligns with this person's mindset, reflecting a patient and strategic approach to settling scores.

SPIRALS AND SPRINGS

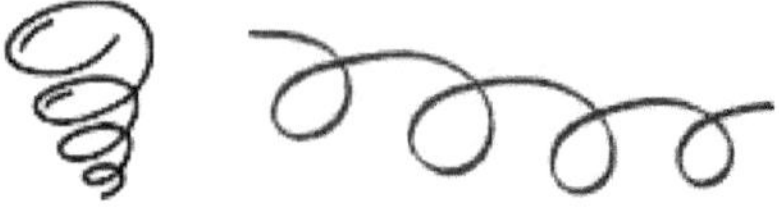

Spirals in Circularity
Spirals often emerge from circular formats, showcasing the flow of expression and optimism. They represent a dynamic and positive outlook on life.

Springs of Tension
When spirals expand like springs, the doodler is infused with tension, poised for the unexpected. It signifies readiness to face challenges head-on.

Interwined Despair
If spirals in your doodle are intertwined or decreasing in size, it may indicate overwhelming feelings. This suggests that challenges or circumstances might be too much for the doodler, reflecting a state of depression or a negative outlook.

FRAMES

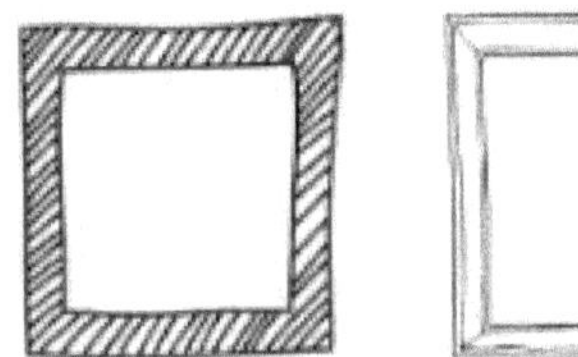

Fence of Torn Desires

Frames or borders around a doodle create a metaphorical fence, symbolizing a conflict within the doodler. It reflects a tug-of-war between the desire for freedom and the inner need for basic protection and security.

Gaps as Windows to Caution

A fence with gaps suggests a cautious approach. The presence of light, hesitant lines without gaps indicates an individual who approaches situations with careful consideration.

Orderly Strokes of Security

Frames with quick, firm strokes and a well-constructed doodle inside portray an orderly and systematic approach. It signifies a desire for structure and a sense of control.

Cross Divisions for Security

A frame with cross divisions inside communicates a deep-seated desire for protection and security. The divisions serve as a symbolic reinforcement, emphasizing the need for stability.

NAMES

Ego in the Signature

Doodling your name or signature frequently suggests a strong sense of ego. It indicates that you often find yourself at the center of your thoughts. If the name is encircled, it may signify additional concerns about someone with that name.

Young Hearts and Names

Youngsters doodling their own names or signatures is a common expression of self-discovery and identity exploration. Comparing their ordinary signature with the doodled version can provide insights into their evolving self-perception.

The Tale of Initials

Doodling names or initials unveils who occupies your thoughts the most. The act of doodling, whether artistically styled or simple lettering, becomes a visual testament to the people who hold significance in your life.

Size Matters

The size of the doodle can be a subtle communicator of importance. Larger doodles may signify individuals of greater significance in your thoughts and emotions.

ASPIRATIONAL DOODLES

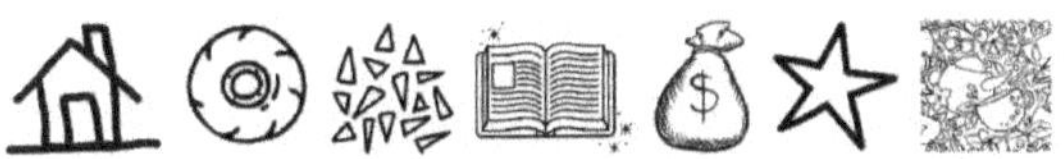

HOUSES

Symbol of Security

Doodling houses symbolizes a deep-rooted desire for safety and security. The level of detail in the drawing reflects the doodler's idealistic tendencies. A well-drawn house indicates a positive outlook on home life, while a messy or asymmetrical representation may signify underlying issues.

Path to the Door

The presence and length of a path leading to the door reveal insights into the doodler's nature. A short path signifies a settled disposition, while a longer path may suggest guardedness. These doodles often mirror one's feelings about home life.

Windows

Windows act as portals to openness and willingness to interact with others. The absence of windows may signify feelings of unhappiness or entrapment.

Hilltop Dwellings

Houses perched on hilltops suggest loneliness or isolation, reflecting the doodler's emotional state.

Chimney Smoke

Smoke rising from a chimney symbolizes a warm and comforting atmosphere inside the house. It signifies a positive sign of coziness.

Roof as Imagination

The roof represents the realm of imagination and new ideas. Its condition, whether complete, tiny, or on fire, reflects the doodler's relationship with their imaginative and fantasy life.

Boundaries and Ego Strength

Lines and walls in the drawing represent the boundaries and strength of the ego. Weak or thin lines suggest vulnerabilities, while strong lines indicate a need to reinforce boundaries.

Doors, Windows, and Pavements

These elements symbolize ways in which others enter or perceive the house. Open doors or many windows may indicate a strong desire for social engagement.

Cars or Boats

The presence of vehicles could signify visitors arriving or individuals leaving the home.

Openness and Exhibitionism

Open doors and large windows, especially in private spaces like the bathroom, may suggest a strong need for interaction or even exhibitionist tendencies.

WHEELS

Mental Alertness
A well-drawn wheel that differentiates from ordinary circles signifies mental alertness and attentiveness.

Direction of Rolling
The direction in which the wheel is depicted rolling carries significant meaning. Rolling forward suggests independence and a forward-looking mindset, while rolling backward indicates a preoccupation with past achievements or glories.

Symbol of Happiness
Individuals who frequently draw wheels and spines tend to possess an inherently happy nature.

STEPS AND LADDER

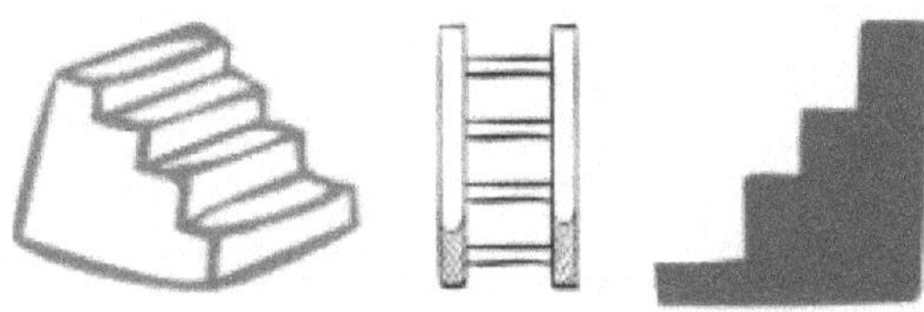

Ambition and Potentially Sexual Symbolism
Doodled steps and ladders hint at an ambitious nature and, in some cases, may carry sexual undertones when drawn quickly with heavy pressure.

Dead-End Reflections
If the steps lead to a dead end, it suggests that the doodler's plans may face obstacles and require reconsideration.

Side-by-Side Steps
Side-by-side steps reveal a flexible personality, resilient in the face of failure, and always ready to embark on a new attempt.

Ladders
Doodled ladders signify progress toward a goal. The style of the ladder reflects the doodler's attitude - confident lines denote assurance, while shaky or uneven lines reveal uncertainty.

TRIANGLES

Aggression, Ambition, and Energy

Triangles in doodles carry the weight of aggression, ambition, and a burst of energy. They symbolize the doodler's driving force and determination.

Sexual Symbolism

For many, triangles also serve as a sexual symbol, representing male genitalia. Heavy pressure in the doodle suggests a mind that is constructive, perceptive, and willing to make sacrifices for personal ambitions.

BOOKS

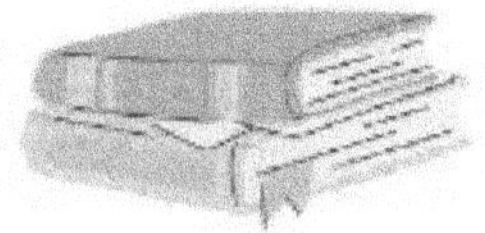

Open Books of Knowledge
Doodled open books signify a genuine interest in expanding one's knowledge and exploring the realms of learning.

Closed Books
Closed books reveal a similar thirst for knowledge but also suggest the ability to keep secrets - a balance between curiosity and discretion.

Series of Books
Interpretation: A series of books communicates methodical and orderly tendencies, possibly hinting at a touch of showmanship.

MONEY

Craving for Comfort

Doodled representations of money signify a desire for more material wealth and the comforts and security it provides.

Greed or Selfish Ambitions

Interpretation: When the doodles extend to the symbols or signs of money, it suggests a degree of greed or selfishness, indicating a focus on personal gains.

STARS

Success and Rule-Bending

Stars in doodles signify an ambitious nature, suggesting a determination to succeed even if it means bending a few rules along the way.

Optimism in Constellations

A bunch of small stars indicates optimism, showcasing a positive outlook and a belief in the potential for multiple achievements.

Singular Goals and Focus

A single, prominent star suggests a singular goal that stands out over others, reflecting a focused and dedicated approach.

Organized vs. Chaotic Stars

Organized and uniform stars indicate focus and dedication, while chaotic and asymmetrical stars reflect an energetic free-thinker.

Harmony and Orientation

Different types of stars, like 5-point and 6-point stars, convey meanings such as harmony and objective orientation.

Yearning for Attention and Signs of Depression

Drawing stars to be the center of attention may reveal a desire for recognition. Conversely, if stars are drawn with too many points or separately, it could indicate struggles with depression.

PATTERNS

Symmetry and Organization
Symmetrical patterns in doodles suggest an organized mind. The more precise the symmetry, the better the executive power.

Complexity as a Measure
The complexity of a doodle serves as a measure of the writer's executive prowess. More intricate patterns imply a heightened ability to manage complexity.

Shading and the Drive Factor
When shading is incorporated into patterns, it may indicate a potential lack of drive or motivation in the writer.

Leadership Traits from Random Patterns
Those who consistently doodle random patterns are believed to grow up as leaders, suggesting a connection between the act of doodling and the development of leadership qualities.

ARROWS

Ascending Arrows

Arrows or ascending straight lines in doodles symbolize ambitions, aspirations, optimism, and motivation. They also suggest a calculated approach to achieving goals.

Descending Arrows

Arrows pointing downward signify that the negative aspects of the writer's life or concerns currently occupy their thoughts. It's a sign of pessimism, worry, or a feeling of being weighed down.

Series of Lines

A small series of lines close together in a doodle suggests a blunt and no-nonsense personality type.

SEXUALITY AND BODY DOODLES

 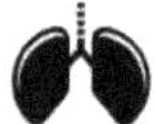   

AEROPLANE

Airplane as a Phallic Symbol
An airplane, when quickly drawn with light pressure, can be seen as a phallic symbol, reflecting subconscious thoughts related to sexuality or personal desires.

Airliner Yearnings
A drawing of an airliner suggests a desire to escape. The writer may be anticipating a holiday or reflecting on one that has recently concluded.

Warplane Connotations
A warplane in a doodle signifies elements of violence or aggression in the writer's thoughts.

Helicopter of Indecision
A helicopter in a doodle implies indecision on the part of the writer. It may reflect uncertainty or a feeling of being in limbo.

BODY PARTS

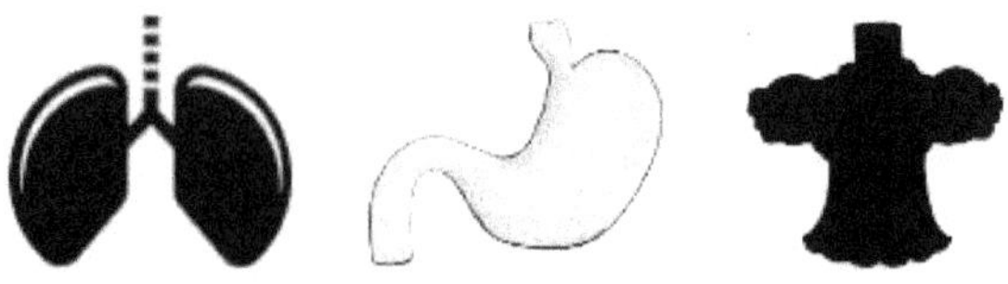

Continuous Drawings
The repetition of drawing specific body parts indicates a heightened interest or focus on that particular area.

Health Matters in Older Individuals
In older individuals, persistent doodles of certain body parts might be linked to health considerations related to those areas.

Sexual Exploration in the Young
In younger individuals, these doodles may have sexual undertones, representing a form of sexual exploration or curiosity.

Gender-Specific Doodles
Adolescents may unconsciously draw body parts associated with their developing gender identity.

EYES

Self-Centered Nature
Doodles of eyes often reflect a self-centered nature, where
the individual may be focused on themselves or their internal
thoughts.

Sexual Connotations
The way eyes are drawn can convey various meanings, from
flirtatiousness to sexual implications.

Symbolism of Female Genitalia
The pressure applied while drawing eyes can carry
symbolism, with light pressure on outer circles and heavier
pressure on the pupil symbolizing female genitalia.

Need for Protection
Geometrically and heavily drawn eyes may suggest a
subconscious desire for protection.

Outgoing Personality
Big eyes in doodles are indicative of an outgoing personality,
suggesting openness and sociability.

Closed Eyes and Refusal to Look Inside
Closed eyes in doodles may signify a reluctance to introspect
or confront inner thoughts and feelings.

SNAKES

Wisdom and Sexual Prowess
Snakes in doodles are often associated with wisdom and sexual prowess, reflecting a blend of intellectual and sensual characteristics.

Phallic Symbolism and Passion
Interpretation: A curving, flowing snake in a doodle is a phallic symbol, representing passion and intense desire.

Coiled Snake: Achievement and Understanding
A snake coiled or upright can symbolize achievement and a deep understanding of one's surroundings. It may also indicate a rebellious and stubborn attitude.

Long and Flexible Snake at Rest: Openness to Suggestion
A snake depicted as long, flexible, and at rest may suggest openness to suggestion and a more adaptable nature.

FRUSTRATION

SQUARES

Aggression and Constructive Ability
Squares in doodles typically signify aggression and a constructive mindset. The individual may be driven to build and create.

Interlocked Squares: Opposition Aversion
Interlocked squares suggest an aversion to opposition. The doodler may prefer order and harmony over conflict.

Squares within Squares: Frustrations and Challenges
Squares drawn within squares may indicate internal frustrations and challenges. The individual might be grappling with unresolved difficulties.

Loosely Drawn Squares: Feeling Trapped
Quickly and loosely drawn squares may signify a feeling of being trapped or confined, suggesting a sense of urgency.

Heavy Pressure Squares: Materialism and Practicality
Squares drawn with heavy pressure can represent materialism and practicality. The individual may value tangible and realistic aspects of life.

FENCES

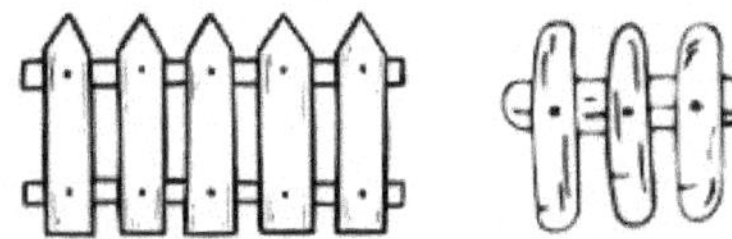

Purpose of Fences: In or Out

Fences in doodles serve as symbolic boundaries. They can represent efforts to keep something in or out, suggesting a need for control or protection.

Fence Surrounding Names

When a fence surrounds a name, it signifies that the person with that name may not be very helpful or might be causing concern.

Round, Stockade Formation: Inhibition

A round or stockade formation of a fence suggests inhibition. The individual may be holding back or feeling constrained in some way.

Geometric Firm Formation: Self-Control

A geometric and firm formation of a fence indicates a sense of self-control. The individual may have a disciplined and measured approach to managing boundaries.

CIRCLES

Completed Circles: Order and Independence
Fully completed circles indicate a desire for order and represent completeness and independence. The individual seeks a sense of wholeness and self-sufficiency.

Incomplete Circles: Flexibility
Incomplete circles suggest a more flexible approach. The doodler may be willing to cooperate but only up to a certain point, showcasing adaptability.

Lazy Streak and Dreaminess
Drawing circles is associated with a lazy streak and a dreamy disposition. The doodler tends to be a visionary, often seeking solutions with minimal effort.

Sexual Symbolism: Female Breasts
Interpretation: Circles drawn with a flowing line that does not join, but ends curling over, symbolize female breasts. This suggests a subconscious connection to sexual themes.

Low Aggression
Circles generally convey very little aggression. The person drawing circles tends to have a calm and non-confrontational nature.

CLOUDS

Small Unshaded Fluffy Clouds: Escapism
Doodling small, unshaded, fluffy clouds suggests a tendency towards escapism. The individual might use imagination or fantasy as a means to escape from reality.

Filled-In Clouds: Emotional and Sexual Challenges
If the clouds are filled in, it indicates difficulty in dealing with emotional and sexual problems. The shaded clouds may represent a clouded emotional landscape.

Series of Clouds: Well-Disposed Personality
A whole series of clouds in various shapes and sizes suggests a well-disposed personality. The doodler may have a positive and open disposition.

Rain Falling from Clouds: Facing Challenges
If rain is shown falling from the clouds, it suggests that the person may spend a lot of time navigating challenges or "crossing bridges" to reach a positive outcome.

DOTS AND SPOTS

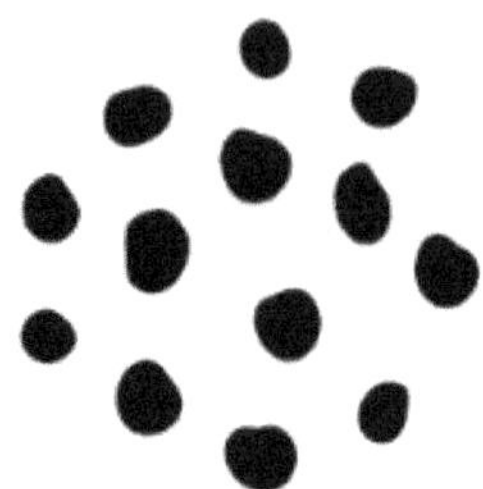

Lots of Dots: Concentration and Focus

Drawings made with lots of dots indicate a strong ability to concentrate and focus. The individual may possess a meticulous and detail-oriented nature.

Linked Dots by Lines: Frustration and Unfulfilled Goals

If dots are linked by lines, it suggests a state of frustration. The person might be grappling with the inability to bring a project or goal to fruition.

Frequent Dots Throughout the Day: Organized Behavior

If someone keeps making dots and spots consistently throughout the day, it signifies organized behavior. The individual is likely sorted and methodical in their actions.

Linked Dots Indicating Trouble or Frustration

If the dots are linked with one another, it suggests that the person is troubled or frustrated.

BOATS AND SHIPS

 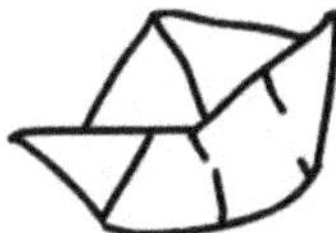 

Ocean Liner: Love for Luxury
Drawing a large ocean liner suggests a deep-seated love for luxury and comfort. The individual might aspire to indulge in the finer things in life.

Speedboats: Adventurous Spirit
Doodling speedboats implies an adventurous nature. The person might have a longing for excitement and thrill in their life.

Sailboats: Dreamer's Expression
Sailboats in doodles indicate a dreamer. The individual may be inclined towards imaginative pursuits and a desire for a life filled with dreams.

Planes, Trains, and Automobiles: Mobility and Escape
Doodles of various modes of transportation like planes, trains, and automobiles represent mobility, movement, or the desire to escape.

Symbol of New Beginnings
Drawing vehicles, including boats, can symbolize an urge for new beginnings. It might reflect a person's aspiration to embark on fresh journeys, whether physical or psychological.

MAZES AND SPIDER WEB

Mazes: Navigating Inner Conflict
Doodling a maze or a web-like pattern suggests the presence of inner conflict. The individual might be grappling with a sense of frustration due to perceived obstacles or a lack of clear direction.

Spider Webs: Feeling Trapped or Trapping Others
Drawing spider webs represents a sense of feeling trapped or stuck. However, it doesn't always imply personal entanglement; the doodler might be symbolically expressing a desire to ensnare someone else.

A doodle featuring well-defined spider webs may indicate that the person feels entangled in a situation. On the other hand, if the webs are drawn around a specific object or figure, it could signify a wish to influence or control that aspect.

BRICK WALL

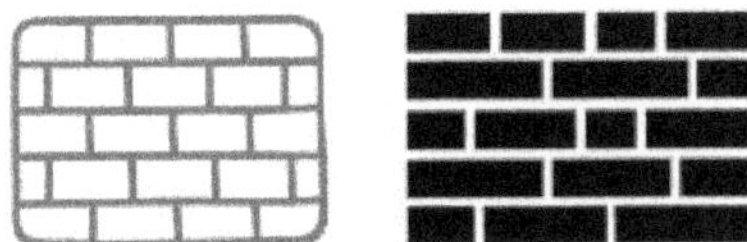

Symbolism of a Brick Wall: Obstacles and Restrictions
Doodling a brick wall suggests a feeling of being blocked or restricted. The tightly packed arrangement of bricks indicates the presence of obstacles hindering progress.

Brick Arrangement: Unraveling Associations
The way the bricks are arranged provides additional insights. Tightly packed or interconnected bricks may indicate a significant obstacle between the individual and their goals.

FIGURES, NUMBERS

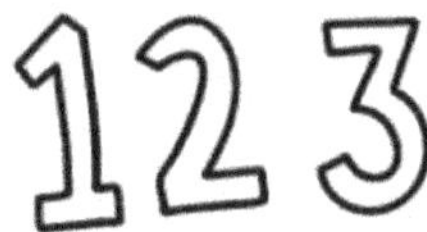

Repetition of Figures: Unveiling Money Troubles
Doodling the same figure repeatedly may signify concerns or preoccupation with financial matters. The repetition might indicate the persistence of money-related problems or the number of entities contributing to the issue.

Number 1: Unraveling the Ego
The number 1, when repeated excessively, may symbolize egocentric tendencies. It suggests a strong focus on the self, potentially leading to a self-centered or individualistic perspective.

OTHER DOODLES

CLOWN

Clown Doodle: Symbolizing Self-Confidence
Drawing a clown in your doodles can be indicative of self-confidence. Clowns are often associated with exuberance, extroversion, and the ability to entertain. The act of doodling a clown suggests a positive self-perception and a certain level of comfort in one's skin.

FEET

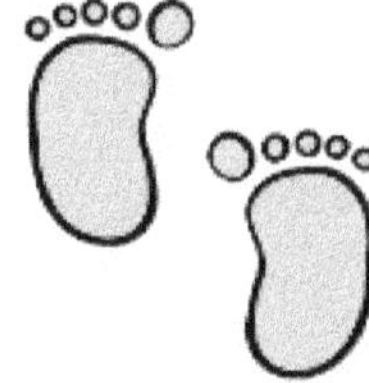

Feet Doodle: Unveiling an Earthy, Passionate Type
Doodling feet can offer insights into the individual's personality. Feet are grounded, and drawing them suggests a down-to-earth, practical nature. The emphasis on directness over romance implies a straightforward and pragmatic approach to life.

FISH

Fish Doodle: Unveiling a Realistic Approach to Matters
Drawing fish in doodles symbolizes a realistic and pragmatic outlook on life. Fish navigate the depths with practicality, and this doodle suggests a similar approach - tackling situations with a keen understanding of the real world.

FIRE OR FLAMES

Fire or Flames Doodle: Embodying Power, Passion, and Momentum
The depiction of fire or flames in doodles is a symbolic representation of power, passion, and the drive to move forward. Flames signify an intense energy that propels the doodler toward their goals, embodying a spirit of fervor and vitality.

EGGS

Eggs Doodle: Symbolizing New Beginnings and the Emergence of Talent
The doodle of an egg holds the profound symbolism of new beginnings and the potential emergence of untapped talents. Eggs, often associated with birth and creation, reflect the embryonic stages of ideas, skills, or endeavors waiting to hatch.

SHOES

Shoes Doodle: Sensual Shapes and Symbolic Expressions
The act of doodling shoes often unveils a person's sensuality and their mode of expression. The shape of the shoe becomes a canvas for unspoken feelings and desires.

Heavy Boot Doodle: The Desire to Dominate
A heavy boot in a doodle serves as a symbolic representation of the desire to dominate. It reflects a sense of authority and a willingness to take charge.

CONCLUSION

"Psychology of DOODLES & SCRIBBLES: Visual Expression of the Unconscious" takes us on a captivating journey through the diverse landscapes of visual expression, unveiling the hidden meanings behind each stroke and curve.

The Journey Within: Navigating the Depths of the Unconscious
From the intricacies of positions and pressures to the nuances of colors and emotions, the exploration begins with a profound understanding of the 'what,' 'when,' 'why,' and 'where' of doodles. The reader is invited to delve into the depths of the mind, where every doodle becomes a silent storyteller, narrating tales of aspirations, frustrations, and the dynamic dance of emotions.

A Symphony of Symbols: Types and Positions
The symphony continues as the book explores the diverse types of doodles, each a unique note in the melody of self-expression. Whether left, right, center, upper, or lower on the page, the position of a doodle becomes a canvas for the subconscious to paint its emotions. The pressure applied, whether heavy or light, adds depth to the symphony, creating a visual language that speaks volumes about the inner world of the doodler.

Nature Unveiled: Trees, Waves, and Hearts
Nature weaves its tapestry in the doodler's mind, with trees representing inner nature, waves echoing the emotional tides, and hearts laying bare the vulnerability near the surface. Each stroke becomes a reflection of the doodler's soul, a visual echo of their hopes, fears, and desires.

Symbolic Sojourn: From Arrows to Zealous Stars

The journey continues through a symbolic sojourn, decoding the meaning behind arrows pointing to ambitions and stars mapping ambitious skies. Boxes, animals, spirals, and springs intertwine to form a rich lexicon, a visual dictionary of the mind's intricate language.

Home and Horizon: Houses and Wheels

Doodling the home unveils a window into inner security, while wheels express the dynamics and mindset of the doodler. Steps become a metaphor for ambition and adaptability, triangles unravel layers of aggression and energy, and books open portals to wisdom and knowledge.

Visual Odyssey: Boats, Mazes, and Beyond

The odyssey expands to boats symbolizing a desire to escape, mazes revealing inner conflicts, and brick walls reflecting obstacles in the path. Figures, numbers, and other doodles add numerical narratives to the visual language, enriching the canvas of the mind.

Playful Persona: Clown, Feet, Fish, and Flames

In the final chapters, the playful persona of a clown, the grounded symbolism of feet, the realistic approach through fish, and the dynamic energy of fire or flames serve as a fitting crescendo. Each doodle becomes a brushstroke in the portrait of the doodler's psyche.

The Unseen Becomes Seen: A Visual Symphony of the Mind

As the curtain falls on this exploration of doodles, the unseen becomes seen, and the visual symphony of the mind resonates in the reader's consciousness. "Psychology of DOODLES & SCRIBBLES: Visual Expression of the Unconscious" is not just a book; it is a journey into the realms of self-discovery, a guide to deciphering the silent language written on the canvas of the unconscious mind.

Saurabh Avasthi, CoFounder – Astrometry

✹ Meet Saurabh Avasthi: Illuminating Lives Through Wisdom and Insight ✹
Saurabh Avasthi stands as an exceptional figure, weaving together the realms of wisdom, transformation, and self-discovery. With a multifaceted journey that spans diverse disciplines, he emerges as a luminary in the realm of holistic coaching and psychological astrology.

☾ Bridging Psychology and Astrology: A Trailblazer in the Field ☾
Saurabh Avasthi wears the crown of being the nation's sole practitioner of Psychological Astrology. Through his unparalleled insight, he delves into the depths of astrology, transcending conventional boundaries. His profound understanding of the human psyche has brought forth a unique perspective that goes beyond predictions – it's about unraveling the intricate tapestry of the mind.

✮ A Catalyst for Transformation and Empowerment ✮
With a legacy of coaching and mentoring thousands, Saurabh's expertise extends beyond astrology. As a seasoned practitioner of Graphology, he deciphers the nuances of written expression. He has become the most sought-after guide in the realm of Vedic Numerology, unraveling the cosmic code of numbers for those who seek clarity and purpose.

⧉ Navigating the Mind's Labyrinth ⧉
Saurabh's credentials extend to the realm of neuro-linguistic programming (NLP). As a certified Master Practitioner, he explores the intricate connections between language, behavior, and transformation. His journey also extends into the realm of hypnotism, where he harnesses the power of the subconscious mind to facilitate change.

♌ Pioneering Research and Unveiling Horoscope Insights ♌
In a quest to understand the intricate interplay between neurocognitive behavior, neuroplasticity, and astrological patterns, Saurabh Avasthi is at the forefront of pioneering research. He envisions a future where science and

spirituality harmonize, offering profound insights into how our horoscopes may shape our cognitive journeys.

💡 From Corporate Heights to Holistic Calling 💡
Saurabh's journey is an embodiment of transformation. After two decades of thriving in the corporate world, steering the realms of Sales and Marketing for esteemed entities such as Colgate Palmolive, Vodafone, Hindustan Times, and Askmebazaar, he embarked on a path fueled by passion. His corporate acumen now synergizes with his spiritual calling, creating a unique blend of practicality and profound insight.

📊 Analytics that Illuminate Pathways 📊
Beyond his spiritual endeavors, Saurabh Avasthi also illuminates pathways through data. He spearheads the realm of Data Analytics with his venture, pdobia (predictive date of birth insights and analytics), fusing ancient wisdom with modern analytics to unveil hidden patterns and potentials.
In essence, Saurabh Avasthi is not merely a coach or an astrologer - he's a torchbearer of transformation, an alchemist of the mind, and a guardian of profound insight. His journey is an invitation to unravel the mysteries of the self and embrace the boundless potential that resides within.

Meenakshi Awasthi, CoFounder – Astrometry

🌟 Discover the Multi-Faceted Magic of Meenakshi Awasthi 🌟
Meenakshi Awasthi is a force of inspiration, seamlessly blending diverse realms into a harmonious tapestry of wisdom, healing, and empowerment. With a journey that traverses the intricate pathways of education, passion, and profound insight, she stands as a guiding light for those seeking clarity and transformation.

📖 Education Meets Creative Expression 🎨
An accomplished Chartered Accountant by education, Meenakshi's journey expands far beyond the numbers. With a passion that ignites her creativity, she is a Qualified Fashion Designer, adding an artistic flair to her repertoire. Yet, her journey doesn't stop here.

🔮 A Journey into the Mystical 🔮
Meenakshi Awasthi seamlessly embodies the mystical arts. As a Pranic Healer, her touch radiates healing energy, as a Palmist, she deciphers the intricacies of one's life imprinted on their hands, and as a Face Reader and Tarot Reader, she unravels the unspoken stories etched on visages and cards.

📜 A Renowned Guide and Teacher 📜
Meenakshi's proficiency extends to the role of a revered teacher. She imparts the art of Palmistry, Face Reading, and Tarot Card Reading through specialized workshops. In her quest to bring holistic wellness, she delves into EFT (Emotional Freedom Technique), Switchwords, Chakra Healing and Balancing, Crystal Healing, and Cord Cutting. Notably, she shares her wisdom through free Meditation sessions, creating spaces of tranquility and rejuvenation for all.

🌿 Healing the Mind, Body, and Soul 🌿
Her journey towards healing is marked by milestones of accomplishment. Meenakshi's expertise spans Basic and Advanced Psychotherapy, Psychic Self Defence, Pranic Facelift, Crystal Healing, and the esteemed levels of Arhatic and ACPH in Pranic Healing. Her dedication to these practices exemplifies her commitment to fostering holistic well-being.

Meenakshi's transformative journey took a courageous turn when she chose to leave a thriving fashion business behind. Her passion for guiding and helping people embarking on their life journeys led her to explore the realms of Palmistry and Tarot. For over five years, she has been a beacon of hope, guiding individuals out of the shadows of depression and agony. Through her unparalleled mastery in predictive palmistry and profound understanding of Tarot, she illuminates the way to positivity and light.

Meenakshi Awasthi has not only identified the precise areas that need healing but has also nurtured countless souls through Pranic Healing and compassionate counseling. Her journey is a testament to the power of passion, the magic of insight, and the boundless potential of healing.

Step into the realm of Meenakshi's wisdom, and let her illuminate your journey with light, healing, and guidance.

✹ Discover Astrometry: Where Wisdom Meets Innovation ✹
Welcome to Astrometry, your portal to a world of wisdom and innovation. Founded by Saurabh Avasthi and Meenakshi Awasthi, Astrometry is not just an institution; it's a transformative journey. With a comprehensive range of courses, groundbreaking software, and a unique consultation platform, we're redefining holistic learning.

Courses That Transform Lives

★ Astrology: Decode cosmic influences shaping destinies.
🔢 Numerology: Unveil the secrets hidden within numbers.
♎ Tarot Card Reading: Tap into the mystic world of symbolism.
✎ Graphology: Master the art of handwriting analysis.
✹ Palmistry: Read the narratives etched on your hands.
👤 Face Reading: Decode personality from facial features.
📚 Philosophy: Embark on a quest for meaning.
❆ Spirituality & Meditation: Connect with your inner self.
☐ Psychology & NLP: Understand the human mind.
❆ Healing Modalities: Harness energies for well-being.
Our Innovative Software
💡 Seamlessly integrating astrology and numerology.
📊 Simplifying complex calculations for accurate insights.
🌐 Empowering seekers to navigate life's journey.
Astrometry Talk - Your Bridge to Wisdom
💬 Connect with experts in astrology, numerology, and more.
☐ Seek solutions and share your wisdom.
💰 Earn through consultations while making a difference.
❆ Holistic Education & Support
🪶 Blend of education, technology, and opportunities.
✹ Empower yourself personally and professionally.
💡 Enhance your life with knowledge from Astrometry.

Join us at Astrometry and unlock your potential.

Where knowledge meets prosperity.

COURSES IN OCCULT AND ESOTERIC SCIENCES

Courses in Astrology
Parashari Astrology
Nadi Astrology
Grad Astrology Courses (Integrated Course of Nadi and Parashari Astrology)
Ayurveda (Medical) Astrology
9 Days 9 Planets
Zodiac and Human Behavior
Nakshatras - Stellar Insights
Mantra Siddhi
Remedies
Yantra Siddhi
Astro Vastu
Moksha Karma and Astrology

Courses in Numerology and Business Science
Essence of Numerology
Advance Predictive Vedic Numerology
Name Numerology
Mobile Numerology
Business /Corporate Numerology
Logo Designing
Visiting Card Designing
Wristwatch Analysis
Business Coach - Integrated Business Training

Courses in Graphology
Master Practitioner Graphology
Signature Analysis
Doodles and Scribbles
Parenting and Child Behavior
Success and Handwriting
Love Betrayal and Handwriting
Money Consciousness and Handwriting

Courses in Palmistry
Predictive Palmistry
Street Smart palmistry
Palmistry and Relationships
Palmistry and Health
Palmistry and Money
Palmistry and Career

Courses in Tarot Card Reading and Face Reading
Tarot Card Reading - Basic to Advance Level
Spreads and Spells
Predictions without learning the meaning
Face Reading
Face Reading basic
Face Reading Advance
Body Language

Other Courses
7-Days 7-Chakras
SwitchWords
Advance Crystals Course
Basic Crystal Course
21- Days Gratitude Course
Animal Totem
Vedic Switchwords
Dowsing
Sigil
Zibu Symbols
Ram Shalaka Prashnavali
Durga Prashnavali

COURSES IN HEALING MODALITIES
Pranic Healing Basic
Pranic Healing Advance
Psychotherapy
Angel Healing Basic
Angel Healing Advance
EFT
Cord Cutting
Crystal Healing
Chakral Healing
Akashic Records
Auto Writing
Access Bar Healing

COURSES IN PSYCHOLOGY
NLP Practitioner Course
Brain : Understanding the Cognitive Journey
Neuro Plasticity : Rewiring Your Brain
Memory and Cognition
Personality Theories
Motivation and Emotions
Self - Hypnosis
Covert - Hypnosis
Psychology for Self Help

Art of Asking Questions
Anger Management
Time Management
Stress Management
Leadership Styles
Habits Formation and Change
Limiting Beliefs
Elicitation of Values
Applied Psychology
Psychology for Manifestation
Psychometric Tests and Workshops
Your Vision Statement
Wheel of Life
Goal Setting
Discovering Personality Types
Discovering Passion

COURSES IN PHILOSOPHY
Introduction to Indian Philosophy
Vedas and Upanishads
Samkhya Philosophy + Yoga Philosophy
Nyaya and Vaisheshika Philosophy
Mimamsa Philosophy
Advaita Vedanta Philosophy
Jain Philosophy
Buddhist Philosophy
Carvaka Philosophy
Contemporary Indian Philosophical Thought
Comparative Study of Indian and Western Philosophies

COURSES IN SPIRITUALITY
Mindfulness Meditation
Transcendental Meditation
Guided Visualization
Breath Awareness Meditation: Ana Paan : Vipassana Meditation
Chakra Meditation
Sound Bath Meditation
Lessons & Learning From
Bhagwad Geeta
Ashtavakra Geeta

MASTER ALCHEMIST PROGRAM
2 Years Integrated Learning Program
(includes all courses)

Touching Billion Lives

+91-8929127575 , +91-7838133555, +91-7838104104

https://astrometry.in
https://courses.astrometry.in
https://astrometrytalk.com

facebook.com/astrometry.in

Instagram.com/astrometrytallk

Youtube.com/astrometry

Twitter.com/astrometryin

Linkedin.com/company/astrometry

Quora.com/profile/Astrometry-1

astrometrytalk

astrometry